NEW SELECTED POEMS
1964–2000

DOUGLAS DUNN

New Selected Poems
1964–2000

ff

faber and faber

First published in 2003
by Faber and Faber Limited
3 Queen Square London WC1N 3AU
Published in the United States by Faber and Faber Inc.,
an affiliate of Farrar, Straus and Giroux LLC, New York

Photoset by Wilmaset Ltd, Wirral
Printed in England by T J International Ltd, Padstow, Cornwall

A CIP record for this book
is available from the British Library

ISBN 0-571-21527-0

2 4 6 8 10 9 7 5 3 1

To Robbie and Lillias Dunn

Contents

from TERRY STREET

The Patricians

In small backyards old men's long underwear
Drips from sagging clotheslines.
The other stuff they take in bundles to the Bendix.

There chatty women slot their coins and joke
About the grey unmentionables absent.
The old men weaken in the steam and scratch at their rough
    chins.

Suppressing coughs and stiffnesses, they pedal bikes
On low gear slowly, in their faces
The effort to be upright, the dignity

That fits inside the smell of aromatic pipes.
Walking their dogs, the padded beats of pocket watches
Muffled under ancient overcoats, silences their hearts.

They live watching each other die, passing each other
In their white scarves, too long known to talk,
Waiting for the inheritance of the oldest, a right to power.

The street patricians, they are ignored.
Their anger proves something, their disenchantments
Settle round me like a cold fog.

They are the individualists of our time.
They know no fashions, copy nothing but their minds.
Long ago, they gave up looking in mirrors.

Dying in their sleep, they lie undiscovered.
The howling of their dogs brings the sniffing police,
Their middle-aged children from the new estates.

Men of Terry Street

They come in at night, leave in the early morning.
I hear their footsteps, the ticking of bicycle chains,
Sudden blasts of motorcycles, whimpering of vans.
Somehow I am either in bed, or the curtains are drawn.

This masculine invisibility makes gods of them,
A pantheon of boots and overalls.
But when you see them, home early from work
Or at their Sunday leisure, they are too tired

And bored to look long at comfortably.
It hurts to see their faces, too sad or too jovial.
They quicken their step at the smell of cooking,
They hold up their children and sing to them.

Incident in the Shop

Not tall, her good looks unstylised,
She wears no stockings, or uses cosmetic.

I sense beneath her blouse
The slow expanse of unheld breasts.

I feel the draughts on her legs,
The nip of cheap detergent on her hands.

Under her bed, forgotten winter bulbs
Die of thirst, in the grip of a wild dust.

Her husband beats her. Old women
Talk of it behind her back, watching her.

She buys the darkest rose I ever saw
And tucks the stem into her plastic belt.

A Removal from Terry Street

On a squeaking cart, they push the usual stuff,
A mattress, bed ends, cups, carpets, chairs,
Four paperback westerns. Two whistling youths
In surplus U.S. Army battle-jackets
Remove their sister's goods. Her husband
Follows, carrying on his shoulders the son
Whose mischief we are glad to see removed,
And pushing, of all things, a lawnmower.
There is no grass in Terry Street. The worms
Come up cracks in concrete yards in moonlight.
That man, I wish him well. I wish him grass.

On Roofs of Terry Street

Television aerials, Chinese characters
In the lower sky, wave gently in the smoke.

Nest-building sparrows peck at moss,
Urban flora and fauna, soft, unscrupulous.

Rain drying on the slates shines sometimes.
A builder is repairing someone's leaking roof.

He kneels upright to rest his back.
His trowel catches the light and becomes precious.

From the Night-Window

The night rattles with nightmares.
Children cry in the close-packed houses,
A man rots in his snoring.
On quiet feet, policemen test doors.
Footsteps become people under streetlamps.
Drunks return from parties,
Sounding of empty bottles and old songs.
The young women come home,
The pleasure in them deafens me.
They trot like small horses
And disappear into white beds
At the edge of the night.
All windows open, this hot night,
And the sleepless, smoking in the dark,
Making small red lights at their mouths,
Count the years of their marriages.

After Closing Time

Here they come, the agents of rot,
The street tarts and their celebrating trawlermen,
Singing or smoking, carrying bottles,
In a staggered group ten minutes before snow.

Winter

Recalcitrant motorbikes;
Dog-shit under frost; a coughing woman;
The old men who cannot walk briskly groaning
On the way back from their watchmen's huts.

The Silences

It is urban silence, it is not true silence.
The main road, growling in the distance,
Continuous, is absorbed into it;
The birds, their noises become lost in it;
Faint, civilised music decorates it.

These are edges round a quiet centre where lives are lived,
Children brought up, where television aerial fixers come,
Or priests on black bikes to lecture the tardy.
If you turn your back on it, people are only noises,
Coughs, footsteps, conversations, hands working.

They are a part of the silence of places,
The people who live here, working, falling asleep,
In a place removed one style in time outwith
The trend of places. They are like a lost tribe.
The dogs bark when strangers come, with rent books, or free
    gifts.

They move only a little from where they are fixed.
Looking at worn clothes, they sense impermanence.
They have nothing to do with where they live, the silence
    tells them.
They have looked at it so long, with such disregard,
It is baked now over their eyes like a crust.

Tribute of a Legs Lover

They are my dancing girls, the wasted lives,
The chorus girls who do not make good,
Who are not given florist's shops or Schools of Dance
By rich and randy admirers, or marry
A gullible Joe from Swindon or Goole,
But find themselves stiff and rotten at fifty,
With bad legs, and no money to pay for the taxi,
Outside cheap drinking places on Grand National day.

Close of Play

Cricketers have the manners of ghosts,
Wandering in white on the tended ground.

They go in now, walking in two's and three's.
This sight is worth a week of evenings.

Players' wives and girlfriends put away tea-flasks,
Start complaining of goosepimples.

Nearby, the vicious pluck of unseen tennis,
A harrier contesting the park its contours,

Fighting a hill with rhythmic blue shoes.
Behind the trees, toughminded fops

In sports cars roar like a mini-Bacchus,
Their girls toss back their summer hair.

The sweet-smelling suburbs cool, settle.
Their people hesitate in the gap before night.

Now it is getting dark, they go indoors.
They do not dance by firelight on their lawns.

Inside, daughters practice one last scale,
Sober sons of teachers learn another fact.

Armchairs surround the tired, the lustful
Absorb their beds. On the garden table,

In the unrotting glasses, dregs of whisky
Or Martini become alive, golden smells.

Gardens aspire to wildness in the dark,
The cricket fields grow defiantly, reach up,

Trees become less polite. The groundsman's roller
Tries to crash screaming into the pavilion.

Out of the webs of ivy, silent as smoke,
Comes the wildness of the always growing,

The menace of unplanned shoots, the brick-eaters.
From taps and cisterns, water, the wild country,

Flows through bungalows and villas.
Damp corners grow moss. The golf course

Becomes a desert, a place without manners.
Rapists gather under hedges and bridges.

[9]

Horses in a Suburban Field

Road-dust settles behind the hedges
That enclose the small suburban fields.
Trees stand in straight lines, planted
By noblemen with an eye for order,
Trees in a park sold off to pay death duty.
Discarded things rot on the ground,
Paper shifts in the wind, metals rust.
Children play in the grass, like snakes,
Out of the way, on headache-soothing absences.

Sad and captured in a towny field,
The horses peep through the light,
Step over the tin cans, a bicycle frame.
They stand under a dried-up hawthorn
With dust on its leaves, smell distant kitchens.
Then they wander through the dust,
The dead dreams of housewives.

Love Poem

I live in you, you live in me;
We are two gardens haunted by each other.
Sometimes I cannot find you there,
There is only the swing creaking, that you have just left,
Or your favourite book beside the sundial.

A Dream of Judgement

Posterity, thy name is Samuel Johnson.
You sit on a velvet cushion on a varnished throne
Shaking your head sideways, saying No,
Definitely no, to all the books held up to you.
Licking your boots is a small Scotsman
Who looks like Boswell, but is really me.
You go on saying No, quite definitely no,
Adjusting the small volume of Horace
Under your wig and spitting in anger
At the portrait of Blake Swift is holding up.
Quite gently, Pope ushers me out into the hell
Of forgotten books. Nearby, teasingly,
In the dustless heaven of the classics,
There is singing of morals in Latin and Greek.

Landscape with One Figure

The shipyard cranes have come down again
To drink at the river, turning their long necks
And saying to their reflections on the Clyde,
'How noble we are.'

Fields are waiting for them to come over.
Trees gesticulate into the rain,
The nerves of grasses quiver at their tips.
Come over and join us in the wet grass!

The wings of gulls in the distance wave
Like handkerchiefs after departing emigrants.
A tug sniffs up the river, looking like itself.
Waves fall from their small heights on river mud.

If I could sleep standing, I would wait here
For ever, become a landmark, something fixed
For tug crews or seabound passengers to point at,
An example of being a part of a place.

South Bank of the Humber

Brickworks, generators of cities, break up
And then descend, sustaining no wages.

A sheet of corrugated iron smacks against a wall,
The wing of a pre-biological, inorganic bird.

It is the laughter of permanence,
The laughter of metal in a brickfield becoming dust.

The Queen of the Belgians

Commemorating Astrid's death
The Belgians made a postage stamp
That my father prized, for her face
Like my mother's, Thirties-beautiful,
Serene around its edges.

I've got it in my album now,
A thing handed down, like advice,
For me to find in the face
Of a queen at Europe's edge
What it was my father found.

Queen Astrid, that my father
Put in an album for her face,
Is puffed into my thoughts by love.
It beats there like the heart of all I know.
I am the age my father was.

Ships

When a ship passes at night on the Clyde,
Swans in the reeds picking the oil from their feathers
Look up at the lights, the noise of new waves
Against hill-climbing houses, malefic cranes.

A fine rain attaches itself to the ship like skin.
The lascars play poker, the Scottish mate looks
At the last lights, one that is Ayrshire,
Others on lonely rocks, or clubfooted peninsulas.

They leave restless boys without work in the river towns.
In their houses are fading pictures of fathers ringed
Among ships' complements in wartime, model destroyers,
Souvenirs from uncles deep in distant engine rooms.

Then the boys go out, down streets that look on water.
They say, 'I could have gone with them,'
A thousand times to themselves in the glass cafés,
Over their American soft drinks, into their empty hands.

A Poem in Praise of the British

Regiments of dumb gunners go to bed early.
Soldiers, sleepy after running up and down
The private British Army meadows,
Clean the daisies off their mammoth boots.
The general goes pink in his bath reading
Lives of the Great Croquet Players.
At Aldershot, beside foot-stamping squares,
Young officers drink tea and touch their toes.

Heavy rain everywhere washes up the bones of British.
Where did all that power come from, the wish
To be inert, but rich and strong, to have too much?
Where does glory come from, and when it's gone
Why are old soldiers sour and the banks empty?
But how sweet is the weakness after Empire
In the garden of a flat, safe country shire,
Watching the beauty of the random, spare, superfluous,

Drifting as if in sleep to the ranks of memorialists
Waiting like cabs to take us off down easy street,
To the redcoat armies, and the flags and treaties
In the marvellous archives, preserved like leaves in books.
The archivist wears a sword and clipped moustache.
He files our memories, more precious than light,
To be of easy access to politicians of the Right,
Who now are sleeping, like undertakers on black cushions,

Thinking of inflammatory speeches and the adoring mob.
What a time would this be for true decadence!
Walking, new-suited, with trim whiskers, swinging
Our gold-knobbed walking sticks, to the best restaurants;
Or riding in closed black carriages to discreet salons,

To meet women made by art, the fashionably beautiful;
Or in the garden, read our sonnets by the pool,
Beside small roses, next week's buttonholes.

In this old country, we are falling asleep, under clouds
That are like wide-brimmed hats. This is just right.
Old pederasts on the Brighton promenade
Fall asleep to dream of summer seductions.
The wind blows their hats away, and they vanish
Into the archives of light, where greatness has gone,
With the dainty tea cup and the black gun,
And dancing dragoons in the fields of heaven.

Cosmologist

There is something joyful
In the stones today,
An inorganic ringing
At the roots of people.

The back of my hand
With its network of small veins
Has changed to the underside of a leaf.
If water fell on me now
I think I would grow.

from THE HAPPIER LIFE

The River through the City

The river of coloured lights, black stuff
The tired city rests its jewels on.
Bad carnival, men and women
Drown themselves under the bridges.
Death-splash, and after, the river wears
Neon flowers of suicides.
Prints of silence ripple where they went in.
An old man rows a black boat and slides past
Unnoticed, a god in an oilskin coat.
He feeds the uncatchable black fish.
They know where Hitler is hiding.
They know the secrets behind sordid events
In Central Europe, in America and Asia,
And who is doing what for money.
They keep files on petty thieves, spies,
Adulterers and their favourite bureaucrats.
That's one old man who's nobody's uncle.
That's one fish you don't want with your chips.
Iron doors bang shut in the sewers.

The Friendship of Young Poets

There must have been more than just one of us,
But we never met. Each kept in his world of loss
The promise of literary days, the friendship
Of poets, mysterious, that sharing of books
And talking in whispers in crowded bars
Suspicious enough to be taken for love.

We never met. My youth was as private
As the bank at midnight, and in its safety
No talking behind backs, no one alike enough
To be pretentious with and quote lines at.

There is a boat on the river now, and
Two young men, one rowing, one reading aloud.
Their shirt sleeves fill with wind, and from the oars
Drop scales of perfect river like melting glass.

The Musical Orchard

Girls on mopeds rode to Fécamp parties,
And as they passed the ripened orchard
Cheered an old man's music,
Not knowing it was sad.
Those French tunes on the saxophone,
The music inside fruit!

Billie 'n' Me

You could never have been a friend of mine,
Even if I played as sweet as dead Lester
Three feet from you, because you mean too much,
Your voice opens all doors on fed-up love.

There were dreams of you, in the ideal night club,
The members gone, just you, the band, and me
In my white tuxedo resisting requests to leave,
Then walking back to my pampered hotel room

In a dawn of fanciful New York heights,
Wondering how you'd take my roses sent at noon,
The invitation to lunch, that you ignored,
The lyrics I had written but you would not sing,

Black, dead, put down by love that was too much,
Mismanaged pleasures. And silent now
As the saxophones in Harlem pawnshops,
Your voice that meant how tough love is.

The Hunched

They will not leave me, the lives of other people.
I wear them near my eyes like spectacles.
Sullen magnates, hunched into chins and overcoats
In the back seats of their large cars;
Scholars, so conscientious, as if to escape
The things too real, the names too easily read,
Preferring language stuffed with difficulties;
And the children, furtive with their own parts;
The lonely glutton in the sunlit corner
Of an empty Chinese restaurant;
The coughing woman, leaning on a wall,
Her wedding-ring finger in her son's cold hand,
In her back the invisible arch of death.
What makes them laugh, who lives with them?

I stooped to lace a shoe, and they all came back,
Mysterious people without names or faces,
Whose lives I guess about, whose dangers tease.
And not one of them has anything at all to do with me.

Modern Love

It is summer, and we are in a house
That is not ours, sitting at a table
Enjoying minutes of a rented silence,
The upstairs people gone. The pigeons lull
To sleep the under-tens and invalids,
The tree shakes out its shadows to the grass,
The roses rove through the wilds of my neglect.
Our lives flap, and we have no hope of better
Happiness than this, not much to show for love
But how we are, or how this evening is,
Unpeopled, silent, and where we are alive
In a domestic love, seemingly alone,
All other lives worn down to trees and sunlight,
Looking forward to a visit from the cat.

from LOVE OR NOTHING

Winter Graveyard

Moss-obelisk and moss-gloved curves
Of uncherishable headstones
Rise from the dead place at the time of death.
A swarm of fissured angels sweeps over
Unremarkable civilians,
Magnates of no inheritance;
In depths of briar and ivy
Their utterly negative remains –
Dried convolvulus,
A bush of nerves sprouted
From lost anatomies.

Survivors of scattered families
Can't get at inscriptions.
When did Frederick die? Or Emily?
They need to know, relatives
Underfoot impart a sad feeling
Worth expeditions
Sometimes beaten back by the strength
Of wild entanglements
Pensioners declare is neglect, unprincipled
Spite of generation for generation,
And imply their own regret.

How can they bear to know they are
Now similarly doomed
In a city not even a metropolis,
And their cross a broken ornament?
Even that era of grand proprieties,
Domain of the picture-hook and claw-footed table,
Its offering servants,
Is sunk and forgotten,

Submerged under midget Gothic;
Fast sycamores grow
Upright out of Victorian creeper.

This is the door to Victoria's heaven.
To sink one's face in a cushion
And share as if from an alms box
Love preserved in Death,
Its hundred-thousand sentiments –
The man who came from the house
With the dancers to talk of the summer,
A soldier who told Edwardian merchants
Of a minor campaign in Assam.
They dance now to secret ragtime
In red-plush joints.

Once they were blue citizenry
At the ends of streets, in horse-traffic.
If I shut my eyes
They are still there, in the same stillness;
The same harmonious dusk
Of a generation whose male children –
Young in 1914 –
Are not buried here
But died abroad defending an Empire's
Affectionate stability
And an industry of lies.

Rank everlastingness
Mud-buttered;
Money is this,
One old penny at the edge of a grave,
Shrill starlings over
Columns and sarcophagi, as many as

Corners hiding God
Here, in his formal dump.
Rubbish of names under vomit of moss;
Inscriptions incised
In thin velvet

Rinse their loving vocabularies
In the light of dreams.
And I am momentarily disabled
By the thought that this is real – pink sky
Behind the black upreaching trees,
Aspirations of beauty and love
Disregarding corroded vulgarity
And farcical monuments
To sanctities not worth the enshrinement
That outlast memory and money.
And a white bird leaves a bare tree.

Winter Orchard

Five days of fog over snow,
Thinning, thickening, thinning
Before dark,
Its last substantial grit,
A breath with industry on it.

Blank miseries
Of the average dead;
Miscellaneous, unspectacular visitation;
Spiritual dregs
Out of the gutters of what-drab-Heaven,

The City of what-suburbanly-managerial-God?
Cold torpor of questions,
Revenge of the unfructified,
Yesterday,
The ash that looks like air.

Emerging, sailing,
Unrescuable grey-drenched browns
Of unpruned apple trees,
Their crush of twigs;
Threat of unleafed forks.

An apple is still stuck there,
Almost yellow in this light.
One survivor of harvest;
Unreachable,
It flourished but came to nothing.

Best efforts are negative,
Seriously beautiful, like art.
Clear light speaks valediction;
Sparse branches
In an orchard of goodbyes,

So many lines that spume or trail off
Beyond limits, their own reaches.
The sky is a net of black nerves,
Continued dream-lines of trees.
Fog's majesty,

Sheer strength of numbers, departs;
Swish of moth-eaten cloaks,
Coarse garments —
Generation upon labouring generation
Of conscripts and grocers' assistants,

Millhands, the unnamed courtiers
Of long-dead industrial magnates.
Their souls shine
On wet slates in summer, sliced turn
Of an autumn furrow, a now-sacred pippin,

As the snow melts like white grease
And soot-spotted stalactites vanish
In their own directions
To destinations that are sounds and wetness;
A soft, cold world
That grows dark when fog clears,
The ground that receives the apple.

In the Small Hotel

There they must live for ever, under soft lights,
The cheated at their favourite separate tables,
Inactive thirds of tender adulteries.

They stare into a light that is always evening,
Their eyes divided, as if distracted by
The ghost of something only one eye sees

Sleep-walking in plastic darkness
Around the night-clubs. They sit like chessmen
At their white round squares, waiting to be moved.

No one makes conversation. A hand
May absently arrange roses in a vase
Or wave away the leering gypsy fiddler.

Chefs please no one there and the waiters stamp
Untipped among customers too vague and lost
To ever think of coming back to commerce.

People we did not want or could not keep;
Someone did this to them, over and over
Wanting their unhappiness until it happened.

Over the dewy grass with a small suitcase
Love comes trotting and stops to hold on a shoe.
To go away with *her*! To drive the limousine

With contraceptives in the glove compartment
Beside the chocolates and packaged orchid
And find that new Arcadia replacing Hollywood!

Remote and amatory, that style of life
In which no one offends or intrudes.
They might as well live in their wardrobes.

Renfrewshire Traveller

Home rain, an aerial night-Clyde,
Spray of recollection
And my only appropriate welcome.

Have I come back?
It was dark
Through Kilmarnock,

Johnny Walker blinked
Imperfectly; history
Is whisky, *lacrimae rerum*.

Have I come back?
I am Scots, a tartan tin box
Of shortbread in a delicatessen of cheddars

And southern specialties.
I am full of poison.
Each crumb of me is a death,

Someone you never see again
After funerals in the rain.
Men who return wearing black ties,

Men who return having looked for work –
Hear them, their Glasgow accents
In the night of high-rise

Skyward tenements, railway platforms,
Accents of rain and arguments.
What have I come to?

Not this. Not this
Slow afright over rails,
This ache in a buffet of empty beer-cans.

This wiping of windows to see a city
Rise from its brilliant lack,
Its fixtures in transparent butter.

Not this visitor
To a place of relatives,
A place of names.

Unlucky Mariners

Clapped out, with long necks
And thin bodies pivoting
On paunches,
They sit like unstrung banjos
Waiting their names to be called.

I dream of rusting hulks
In the Indies,
Jammed among the mangrove
Where sea stops inch by inch,
Water, snakes and vegetable are one.

'John Rigg, you spilled your rum
From Stornoway to the dreary Plate.
I saw you wench Malacca
Under the palms;
You changed your ladies with the tide.'

Dance of the shingle resort,
Fore-shore trash
And harbour-masters counting
Prosperity by tonnage –
Here are the makers of music,

The numbers missed by arithmetic,
Unshipped and down on their luck
As they have been down on their luck
In disgusting jails
Near all the harbours.

'MacBryde, you shipped out of Glasgow
In '32, and you're back
With five German duckings
And thoughts of as many bastards
As you've had slit-skirted slope-eyed whores.'

Once, on a raft on a lagoon
Of Renfrewshire's Clyde,
An old man waved from his freighter;
He had nothing to do but wave to me,
And I thought, 'I'll go to sea.'

I dream of rusting hulks
And undersea
The leaky tubs that God's torpedo
Plugged; in South Pacific huts
The lucky mariners, copra kings

With four wives and the respect
Of The Islands,
Playing much-repaired concertinas
Long into the night,
To the tropical stars.

And I look at this lot,
Calling out their names
From *The Ledger of Missing Seafarers*,
So seldom called
They think I call their fathers.

Their grey skins are radiant mist,
Their eyes deep pools
In which monsters sleep –
From nautical boyhoods
To skeletal service on The Ghost Ship.

'Falkenberg, you've a lot
To answer for. Your slummy crew
Picked off the bobbing wrecks
Might answer to your bells
But you're shipless now.'

Wrecks of many seas,
Here by the silent shipyards
Of the shore, ghosts of nuts and bolts
Toast your epiphanies
In the transparent grave of the fish.

Caledonian Moonlight

The white moon opens over a ridge of bracken
Spilling its prodigal rays into the eyes
Of the last pair of wildcat in the county
Looking for the kittens of their sterility
In the wiry heather

And the beautiful white face of a secretary
Rises in the shut eyes of a bachelor caretaker
Whose mother is dreaming
Of handing a plate of sandwiches to the minister

There are more moons in the night
Than eyes of those who see them
Open, venereal

Going to Bed

Free as the frequent rain,
And our footprints rise from their deepest marks
Till the globe is smooth of us again.

'Mundus senescit' says my priest.
The world grows old in moonlight.
And more than that, the world was always old.

Love, who is warm?
Even at this hour, the motorbikes
Gurgle their vehemences,

All-night taxis huddle round the telephone,
Sonorous locomotives pull away from time
Into the night of may-blossom,

Night that subdues the verticals
And leaves the world flat, its floating lights
Pulsing, excited hearts of predators.

Once, to a girl, I said, 'Hell is hard.
Forget me. That's easy.' And was that bad?
But being bored is full of such surprises.

And now we fly, not mattering much,
And only then to you and I,
Pale ecstasisers in a glade of rooms

When just by looking we can see our minds
Or with our fingers turn the moon
Of this excited May, to see its other side,

The Apple-Island and our carnal truth
Hushed out of its confusion by
Physical orchards, slowed rush of waves.

I Am a Cameraman

They suffer, and I catch only the surface.
The rest is inexpressible, beyond
What can be recorded. You can't be them.
If they'd talk to you, you might guess
What pain is like though they might spit on you.

Film is just a reflection
Of the matchless despair of the century.
There have been twenty centuries since charity began.
Indignation is day-to-day stuff;
It keeps us off the streets, it keeps us watching.

Film has no words of its own.
It is a silent waste of things happening
Without us, when it is too late to help.
What of the dignity of those caught suffering?
It hurts me. I robbed them of privacy.

My young friends think Film will be all of Art.
It will be revolutionary proof.
Their films will not guess wrongly and will not lie.
They'll film what's happening behind barbed wire.
They'll always know the truth and be famous.

Politics softens everything.
Truth is known only to its victims.
All else is photographs – a documentary
The starving and the playboys perish in.
Life disguises itself with professionalism.

Life tells the biggest lies of all,
And draws wages from itself.
Truth is a landscape the saintly tribes live on,
And all the lenses of Japan and Germany
Wouldn't know how to focus on it.

Life flickers on the frame like beautiful hummingbirds.
That is the film that always comes out blank.
The painting the artist can't get shapes to fit.
The poem that shrugs off every word you try.
The music no one has ever heard.

The White Poet
Homage to Jules Laforgue

I've travelled by the ice-floes
Purer than purest first white communicants.
I don't go to church...
I'm the High Chancellor of Insight,
Remember that...

I'm a random harvest of cells,
Thinking, farting, married.
I could have been the perfect husband –
The whispering of her long dress over the carpet
In the next room is a magic hush-hush.

My shoes have walked cobblers' miles
On the backstreets. Rain, and spires of factories
In the rain ... pianos in all the houses –
Agoraphobic furniture drizzle would love to warp.
The keyboard, an international gutter.

Pianos in the prim districts are playing
Tedious waltzes, the music of moderation.
And over the domes of swimming-baths
A clarinet's chalumeau tune drags from subterranean woods
Amazing possibilities of Priapus.

All Saints, Margaret Street, a wedding in a doorway
Touted by photographers, waiting for a cab...
Red-brick palace, streaming, baked,
Naked in its numbered days, hallowing the weddings
Of ill-dressed parties without taxis.

And the melancholy horns! Sad, undersea
Deranged tan-tivvy, dislocated fanfare!
Driven on the North Wind, ta-ra! ta-ta!
Turning the head of the groom who stands
Like a gland ripped from a throat.

Tanneries, chemical works, docks, post offices,
Brassy flourish of work, the diseased architecture –
Fog-flecked spittle solid on the soul.
Nature, stale factory of sap with the frenzied stink,
Is no one in love?

Or is *this* love?
All night, Our Lady of the Evenings
Never makes her mind up. Her leave-takings
Are the swishes of black dresses,
She loves a box of brutal adornments –

A gross Gothic of smoke and bubbling vats,
A Northern torch of furnaces
And Sunday afternoons of business districts
Evaporated of their carnal typists.
Hypochondria and slaughter!

Chattering in the streets, chattering in the shops,
Small talk of commercial companionships –
Where the corner-shop is an off-licence, the delicatessen
Is usually closed. That street is pretty.
This is what is meant by a City. That is the lesson.

And railway stations, breathless at the platform's end –
How lovely to look at, those trains we miss!
Gentlemen, lift the seat! Gone, without me!
Splendid, splendid, to leave the friend
Waiting with his watch in the specified pub.

Moon-woman, lover, I would gladly wring from you
White bodies of the populace
To save them, but you laugh,
Offering your ligature of nebulous caresses,
Pale oddities, mottoes of madness

And nothing to grab hold of. Moon, sick angel
Suspended through stages of globular striptease,
You vanish like love, the personality
Sipped through ice, the woman's lips on her Daiquiri –
Crushed, fragile pink drizzle in blankness.

God so loved the world
He puked every time he looked at it,
With a few miraculous exceptions. He's gone now.
Sundays, and parked cars of visitors, special joints
Like amputated stumps oozing in the ovens.

And it is the day of *The Moderation Waltz* –
    We will not buy the best, *one two three*
    We won't beat our breasts, *one two three*
    And we'll have no truck
    With that muck
    In foreign restaurants, *da-da dum-dum*

[39]

Paupers are swimming through their blood
To meet their other parents at the far end
Where fauntleroys picnic in stable sunshine
And father punts mother on the river
To the crystal honeymoon.

O waves of honey, Moon, perambulators, gloves!
Useful apostrophes!
The world is passionate as insomnia –
Insomnia of power stations sailing
In self-generated glows like bulky saints;

Insomnia of engines that start with a twist;
Insomnia of police forces, watching
Vulnerable depots of money;
Ships on their incessant stagger;
Insomniac clocks, hysterically

Ticking, the tick-tick-tock
And obliging semaphore
On the complaisant eye
Of the clock – punctual, early, late,
And remember you must die.

Sundays, time-locks, vaults, factories –
Over the land of Sunday, my wet love,
I stretch my hand.
What joins us is an ampersand.
It's easier for us. Should I take off my glove?

Should I cry in the streets, or sail over the rooftops –
Silver Street, Holy Trinity, the Guildhall, Whitefriargate –
Dropping leaflets?
Toddle off, my songs; go to the lutes
Of untuned strings, played by God's mutes,

And make no mark, subside with no pock
Or ripple in the sane mud. More dirt, more dirt!
In the botched fog of outcries, the political sandwiches –
The sky is high, and so am I –
Ah, they say, the same neat suit and tidy ties.

from BARBARIANS

'He was bored, but nevertheless he slowly grew further and further away from the hardship and simplicity of the workers, from his childhood environment. He somehow learned how to behave, as they say. Without realizing it, he cut himself off from his own people. ... He thought he was merely bored, but secretly he was flattered at being included. Some forces drew him towards the bourgeoisie; other forces sought to retard his transition.'

'The truth of life was on the side of the men who returned to their poor houses, on the side of the men who had not "made good".'

Paul Nizan, *Antoine Bloyé*

The Come-on

'... the guardian, the king's son, who kept watch over the gates of
the garden in which I wanted to live.'

Albert Camus

To have watched the soul of my people
    Fingered by the callous
Enlivens the bitter ooze from my grudge.
    Mere seepage from 'background'
Takes over, blacking out what intellect
    Was nursed by school or book
Or had accrued by questioning the world.
    Enchanting, beloved texts
Searched in for a generous mandate for
    Believing who I am,
What I have lived and felt, might just as well
    Not exist when the vile
Come on with their 'coals in the bath' stories
    Or mock at your accent.
Even now I am an embarrassment
    To myself, my candour.
Listen now to the 'professional classes'
    Renewing claims to 'rights',
Possession of land, ownership of work,
    Decency of 'standards'.
In the bleep-bleep of versicles, leisure-novels,
    Black traffic of Oxbridge –
Books and bicycles, the bile of success –
    Men dressed in prunella
Utter credentials and their culture rules us,
    A culture of connivance,
Of 'authority', arts of bland recoveries.
    Where, then, is 'poetry'?

Brothers, they say that we have no culture.
    We are of the wrong world,
Our level is the popular, the media,
    The sensational columns,
Unless we enter through a narrow gate
    In a wall they have built
To join them in the 'disinterested tradition'
    Of tea, of couplets dipped
In sherry and the decanted, portentous remark.
    Therefore, we'll deafen them
With the dull staccato of our typewriters.
    But do not misbehave –
Threats and thrashings won't work: we're outnumbered.
    Drink ale if you must still,
But learn to tell one good wine from another –
    Our honesty is cunning.
We will beat them with decorum, with manners,
    As sly as language is.
Take tea with the king's son at the seminars –
    He won't know what's happening.
Carry your learning as does the mimic his face.
    Know one knife from another.
You will lose heart: don't show it. Be patient;
    And sit on that high wall
In its obstacle glass chips, its barbed wire,
    Watching the gardeners.
One day we will leap down, into the garden,
    And open the gate – *wide, wide.*
We too shall be kings' sons and guardians,
    And then there will be no wall:
Our grudges will look quaint and terrible.

In the Grounds
Yorkshire, 1975

Barbarians in a garden, softness does
Approve of who we are as it does those
Who when we speak proclaim us barbarous
And say we have no business with the rose.

Gently the grass waves, and its green applauds
The justice, not of progress, but of growth.
We walk as people on the paths of gods
And in our minds we harmonize them both.

Disclosures of these grounds – a river view,
Two Irish wolfhounds watching on a lawn;
A spinster with her sewing stares at you
And begs you leave her pretty world alone.

More books than prejudice in our young minds…
We could not harm her, would not, would prefer
A noise less military and more kind
Than our boots make across her wide *parterre*.

We are intransigent, at odds with them.
They see our rabble-dreams as new contempt
For England's art of house and leaf. Condemn
Our clumsiness – you do not know, how, unkempt

And course, we hurt a truth with truth, still true
To who we are: barbarians, whose chins
Drool with ale-stinking hair, whose horses chew
Turf owned by watching, frightened mandarins,

Their surly nephews lounging at each gate,
Afraid we'll steal their family's treasured things,
Then hawk them – pictures, furniture and plate –
Round the encampments of our saddle-kings.

Here Be Dragons
Pomponius Mela, Chorographia

In Africa, Pomponius Mela wrote,
Are tribes whose bodies stop below the throat.
His readers might not marvel much at that
Headless and monstrous proletariat
For Mela says that faces on their chests
Had all the usual features and, unless
Pomponius lied, I can suppose their art,
Doubtless oral, came straight from the heart.

There, too, in Africa, were troglodytes
Who housed themselves in the eternal night.
This Mela proffers civilized distaste.
He says of these non-citizens of waste
And downward-tunnelled tenements, they dined
On serpents they discovered as they mined.
But had they raised their tenements through sky,
What lunch would fowl-fed Mela specify?

Mela records a tribe that cursed the sun
At dusk and dawn. These people of No-One
Possessed no names and did not dream. Dreamless
Without nomenclature, did Mela bless
That dreamless people who knew more than he

Could ever know of their reality,
Cursing the sun, cursing at dusk and dawn,
For reasons Romans couldn't lay their fingers on?

These then were wonders Mela thought he saw
In lives reported as hair, skin and claw.
That flattered Rome, to keep its *regnum* sure –
The home of shave and soap and manicure.
One story's left, the one that Mela tells
That's their revenge – the one about the well.
Arriving there, thirsty and out of breath,
Romans might drink, then laugh themselves to death.

Gardeners

England, Loamshire, 1789
A gardener speaks, in the grounds of a great house,
to his Lordship

Gardens, gardens, and we are gardeners...
Razored hedgerow, flowers, those planted trees
Whose avenues conduct a greater ease
Of shadow to your own and ladies' skins
And tilt this Nature to magnificence
And natural delight. But pardon us,
My Lord, if we reluctantly admit
Our horticulture not the whole of it,
Forgetting, that for you, this elegance
Is not our work, but your far tidier Sense.

Out of humiliation comes that sweet
Humility that does no good. We know
Our coarser artistries will make things grow.
Others design the craftsmanship we fashion

To please your topographical possession.
A small humiliation – Yes, we eat,
Our crops and passions tucked out of the view
Across a shire, the name of which is you,
Where every native creature runs upon
Hills, moors and meadows which your named eyes own.

Our eyes are nameless, generally turned
Towards the earth our fingers sift all day –
Your day, your earth, your eyes, wearing away
Not earth, eyes, days, but scouring, forcing down
What lives in us and which you cannot own.
One of us heard the earth cry out. It spurned
His hands. It threw stones in his face. We found
That man, my Lord, and he was mad. We bound
His hands together and we heard him say –
'Not me! Not me who cries!' We took away

That man – remember, Lord? – and then we turned,
Hearing your steward order us return,
His oaths, and how you treated us with scorn.
They call this grudge. Let me hear you admit
That in the country that's but half of it.
Townsmen will wonder, when your house was burned,
We did not burn your gardens and undo
What likes of us did for the likes of you;
We did not raze this garden that we made,
Although we hanged you somewhere in its shade.

The Student
Of Renfrewshire, 1820

For our Mechanics' Literary Club
I study Tacitus. It takes all night
At this rough country table which I scrub
Before I sit at it, by candlelight,
Spreading my books on it. I think respect
Must work like love in any intellect.
    Difficult Latin sticks in my throat
    And the scarecrow wears my coat.

What put me up to it, this partnership
Of lexicon and text, these five books thieved,
These two books borrowed, handed down, this grip
Of mind on mind, this work? Am I deceived?
Is literature a life proved much too good
To have its place in our course neighbourhood?
    Difficult Latin sticks in my throat
    And the scarecrow wears my coat.

In Paisley when they read the Riot Act
We faced the horsemen of the 10th Hussars.
Men's bones were broken, angry heads were cracked –
Provosts, sheriffs, guns and iron bars.
We thrashed the poet William Motherwell,
That depute-sheriff and the law's law-minstrel.
    Difficult Latin sticks in my throat
    And the scarecrow wears my coat.

Between us and our lives were bayonets.
They shone like water. We were crooked with thirst,
That hot dry bubbling when your whole life sweats.
'If you want life', they said, 'you must die first.'

Thus in a drought of fear Republic died
On Linen Street, Lawn Street and Causeyside.
    *Difficult Latin sticks in my throat
    And the scarecrow wears my coat.*

Beneath our banners I was marching for
My scholarship of barley, secret work
On which authority must slam its door
As Rome on Goth, Byzantium on Turk.
I'm left to guess their books, which precious line,
Eluding me, is never to be mine.
    *Difficult Latin sticks in my throat
    And the scarecrow wears my coat.*

Frost, poverty, rare, rare, the rapid rain...
What good can come of study, I must have.
I read it once, then read it twice again.
Fox, whittrick, dog, my horse, my new-born calf –
Let me recite my life, my animals and clay,
My candlelight, my fuddled melody.
    *Difficult Latin sticks in my throat
    And the scarecrow wears my coat.*

Such hard work urges me to turn each line
As firmly as I plough a furrow straight,
By doing so make this work clandestine,
Mix its affections with both love and hate.
So, Tacitus, old friend, though not to me,
Allow me master your authority.
    *Difficult Latin sticks in my throat
    And the scarecrow wears my coat.*

Empires

All the dead Imperia ... They have gone
Taking their atlases and grand pianos.
They could not leave geography alone.
They conquered with the thistle and the rose.
To our forefathers it was right to raise
Their pretty flag at every foreign dawn
Then lower it at sunset in a haze
Of bugle-brass. They interfered with place,
Time, people, lives, and so to bed. They died
When it died. It had died before. It died
Before they did. They did not know it. Race,
Power, Trade, Fleet, a hundred regiments,
Postponed that final reckoning with pride,
Which was expensive. Counting up the cost
We plunder morals from the power they lost.
They ruined us. They conquered continents.
We filled their uniforms. We cruised the seas.
We worked their mines and made their histories.
You work, we rule, they said. We worked; they ruled.
They fooled the tenements. All men were fooled.
It still persists. It will be so, always.
Listen. An out-of-work apprentice plays
God Save the Queen on an Edwardian flute.
He is, but does not know it, destitute.

Watches of Grandfathers

They go with corporations
And with fountain pens,
With honour and inscription,
Fastidious longevities
In which are reckoned
The funerals of friends.

Worn in relation to work,
Timetables, opening times,
And counterparts carried by
Despicable referees,
They are neat in the palm of a hand.
Always to be dangled before

Babies in prams, consulted
With flourishes that invite
Benevolent side-glances,
They have a kindness
Which the artistry of time
In its steady circles

Denies, as it measures
Proximity to pensionable age,
Or, from a safe hook
In the corner of a workshop,
Hung there, stare at the bench
As they mutter 'Death, Death'.

They long for the pocket
Of the eldest son, in
The waistcoat he will buy for one,

Who will see his father's eye
Glazed on it, and the age
Of his sons slowly numbered.

Portrait Photograph, 1915

We too have our place, who were not photographed
So much and then only in multitudes
Rising from holes in the ground to fall into smoke
Or is it newsreel beyond newsreel
But I do not know and I have lost my name
And my face and as for dignity
I never had it in any case, except once,
I think, in the High Street, before we left
For troopships and the farewell pipers,
When it was my turn in the queue
In Anderson's Photographic Arcade and Salon,
In my uniform, and I was not a tall man
Although for a moment I had a sense
Of posterity in the eyes of descendants,
Of my own face in a frame on a small table
Over which her eyes would go, and my sons',
And that I would persist, in day and night,
Fading a little as they say they do.

The Musician

They've told me MacAuley is gone now
Taking his tool-box and both his fiddles.
They are saying, 'What will we do now?
There is no music in this or the next parish.'

Until a replacement is found there
Not one note will be heard after whist
Unless it is played from a record –
That, even the young say, won't be as good.

They will talk of MacAuley for ever there,
Long after their own receipt of pensions,
Of his carpenter's wrist on the fiddle-bow
Stitching like mad through jig-time.

And so I have heard on the telephone
MacAuley is gone now, and both his fiddles
Lie in their cases under the stairs
With the music we never knew he could read.

It is Beethoven and Bach, they tell me,
And a very fat volume, a German tutor,
That cost six shillings before the war,
And its pages, they tell me, are black with notes.

It's your carpenter's wrist they remember
In love with your local tradition.
Your carpenter's fist could not break through
To the public of Bach and Beethoven.

So they've told me MacAuley is gone,
Both his fiddles lie under the stairs now
With music by Bach and Beethoven
Beside six bob's worth of ambition.

Let them open your window frames, open your doors,
Think, as they sit on their mended chairs,
Of you, their musician, and doctor to wood,
That no one has heard what you understood.

Glasgow Schoolboys, Running Backwards

High wind ... They turn their backs to it, and push.
Their crazy strides are chopped in little steps.
And all their lives, like that, they'll have to rush
Forwards in reverse, always holding their caps.

Red Buses
'The last Western'

Galoot and lover, homeward drunks
Through Govan, Linthouse, Renfrew Cross
Have known well the sudden lurch
Of double-deckers to the digestive system.
God help the man who pukes on his seat
Or is tempted to impertinence.
He will have no Requiem.
Nor in the Golf Inn will there be sung
Delicate character studies;
No pawky *éloge* in the Wallace Arms
Nor in the crowds of Glasgow be missed
Among umbrellas and young women in
Greatcoats selling *Morning Star*,
For these are the plain facts of the matter:
No longer will singing be tolerated
Nor the mess created by those

Who cannot hold it in, but who
Must for ever be incontinent.
From now on are conductresses instructed
To put the boot in at the first signs of
Contraventions of these Orders –
And our women, as you know, are worse than our men,
Whose only function is,
In this business, to take prisoners.
Therefore, you who have lost your hearts
In San Francisco or who sing
Of your mother's eyes, take warning...
Already you will have heard how
Sundry gung-ho Yankee submariners
Found themselves airborne at Bishopton.
They walked around, amazed
In the night of council houses.
One we heard of slept in the garden
Of a distinguished JP, waking
Under a coverlet of leaves and dew
To sing sad songs of Ohio
Or wherever it was he came from.
We will no longer brook misbehaviour,
Not even from presbyterians.
So, revise your youths. Forget
Your indiscretions on the back-seat
And the disasters of carry-outs
In paper-bags not strong enough
For the purpose. From now on you will walk home.
If it drives you crazy to listen to
Softly ticking factories; or if
Under the tenements you feel you are
In a Glencoe of the mind; or if
Cranes, shipyards, sleeping it off

In the sweat of forgotten labour
Are better served in peace than you are;
Or if, by the bonded warehouses,
You see the square root of all distillations;
Or if you have forgotten the road
And get lost for ever in the first
Mattress of West-bracken, the first
Gaunt countryside of the West, then that
Is your fault. You will not be alone.

Ballad of the Two Left Hands

When walking out one morning
   Walking down Clydeside Street
I met a man with two left hands
   Who said he was obsolete.

At noon the work horns sounded through
   The shipyards on Clyde's shore
And told men that the day had come
   When they'd work there no more.

Economy is hand and sweat
   A welder in his mask
A new apprentice pouring tea
   From his father's thermos flask.

And soon these men of several trades
   Stood there on Clydeside Street
Stood staring at each new left hand
   That made them obsolete.

'Beware of men in suits,' one said
    'Take it from me, it's true
Their drivel economics'll
    Put two left hands on you.'

All in the afternoon was shut
    When I walked out again
The day had pulled on its black gloves
    And turned its back on men.

I walked the dusk of darkened cranes
    Clyde broke on Clyde's dark shore
And rivets fired where men still work
    Though men work here no more.

High in the night's dark universe
    I saw the promised star
That men I knew raise glasses to
    In an illegal bar.

They toast that city still to come
    Where truth and justice meet
And though they don't know where it is
    It's not on Clydeside Street.

With thumbs stuck on the wrong way round
    In two left-footed shoes
I saw a man search in his heart
    And ask it, 'Are you true?'

That man who sat on Clydeside Street
    Looked up at me and said
'I'll study this, then I'll pick clean
    The insides of my head.'

And moonlight washed the shipyards then
    Each crane was hung with stars
Rinsed in the moonlight we stared up
    Like old astronomers.

Economy is hand and sweat
    And foundrymen and fire
Revise your textbooks, multiply
    Your guilt by your desire.

Such dignity, so many lives,
    Even on Clydeside Street
When mind and heart together ask
    'Why are we obsolete?'

Lost Gloves

I leave my body in a new blue suit
    With my soul, which is newly destitute.
Rinsed spirit of me, washed for this departure,
    Takes off adroitly to its atmosphere.

And here's that blue glove on a railing's tip
    Where iron, frost and wool make partnership
Of animal and elements and blue –
    Lost little glove, I still remember you.

You do not fit my hand now, nor can I fit
    My world with life, nor my mouth match its spit,
My tongue, my words, my eyes the things they see.
    My head is upside down in memory

A child walks to his mother, right hand bare
    And hidden in his coat, then follows her
Inside, his gloved hand on the banister,
    His right hand on his heart, remaining there.

My pulse beats backwards to a street in winter –
    Blue first perceived, that I now disinter
Blue out of blue where life and childhood crossed:
    Five blue wool-fingers waving in the frost.

On Her Picture Left with Him

On trains to London and the south
    And thus away from me
These words in my enamoured mouth
    Summon the flattery
Of who it is and what I love,
    Distracting me.

Lady, so far outside, and gone,
    Your picture left with me
Is like the world I look upon
    And shows reality
As who it is and why I love,
    Distracting me.

Thus do I gaze on you, and drink
    Your face you left with me,
And speak to you in whispered ink
    With that humility
Which is a lesser spoil of love,
    Distracting me.

Now is the afternoon turned round
  To dusk that darkens me,
And walking on nocturnal ground
  Offers no liberty
From who I am and who I love,
  Distracting me.

Old Things

Time and removal vans
Scatter dead widows
From their dying children.
It is late, secretly.
It is a late era
In the grey-stilted rain.
And you who pilfer
In shops of second-hand
Among shabby heirlooms,
Accumulating bits
Of blue pottery, a chair,
A vase, a baby-grand,
Consider – now it's late –
What things come up for air
Out of such furniture,
Whose-hands in the polish,
What-lover's-eye upon
Pendants of amethyst,
Whose-name you wear inside
Whose-bangle on your wrist.

Wedding

Confetti in the gutters,
Half a dozen leaves
That reach here from autumn,
Yearly ... What point is there
In regretting no shrubbery
Or abundance of green
Hallows this couple, when the car
The groom has worked on for weeks
Takes them down a street
Elated by love and community?
There is one season
For poverty, and delight
Overlaps all things.

The Return

'Grey skies are just clouds passing over.'
                          Duke Ellington

The window-cleaner carried
A cloth bag full of change
And it rattled the tariff
Of window-panes.

There are his ladders
Left by the wall.
There is his pail. There is his rag.
But the windows are broken.

Houses are empty
And rusting aerials sing
A congress of metal and wind
And indifferent sparrows.

Gushed soot on the hearths,
Heaps of plaster, split timbers,
Sodden newsprint and wreckage of armchairs
Litter ripped living-rooms.

I imagined perfection.
My dreams have come home
To die here and cling to
My anarchy of convictions.

If only there were no such troubles.
My politics vanished
To the end of the street
Where beauty and pollution meet

In natural ecstasy,
A hint of trees
By the abandoned railway
And a red sunset.

And this is the house I owned,
My two sufficient rooms.
There is no trace of me
As I look for signs

Of 'little jobs' I did about the house,
Domestic, studious, and in love,
Three things, or so I'm told,
I should have fought against.

from ST KILDA'S PARLIAMENT

St Kilda's Parliament: 1879–1979
The photographer revisits his picture

On either side of a rock-paved lane
Two files of men are standing barefooted,
Bearded, waistcoated, each with a tam-o'-shanter
On his head, and most with a set half-smile
That comes from their companionship with rock,
With soft mists, with rain, with roaring gales,
And from a diet of solan goose and eggs,
A diet of dulse and sloke and sea-tangle,
And ignorance of what a pig, a bee, a rat,
Or rabbit look like, although they remember
The three apples brought here by a traveller
Five years ago, and have discussed them since.
And there are several dogs doing nothing
Who seem contemptuous of my camera,
And a woman who might not believe it
If she were told of the populous mainland.
A man sits on a bank by the door of his house,
Staring out to sea and at a small craft
Bobbing there, the little boat that brought me here,
Whose carpentry was slowly shaped by waves,
By a history of these northern waters.
Wise men or simpletons – it is hard to tell –
But in that way they almost look alike
You also see how each is individual,
Proud of his shyness and of his small life
On this outcast of the Hebrides
With his eyes full of weather and seabirds,
Fish, and whatever morsel he grows here.
Clear, too, is manhood, and how each man looks
Secure in the love of a woman who

Also knows the wisdom of the sun rising,
Of weather in the eyes like landmarks.
Fifty years before depopulation –
Before the boats came at their own request
To ease them from their dying babies –
It was easy, even then, to imagine
St Kilda return to its naked self,
Its archeology of hazelraw
And footprints stratified beneath the lichen.
See, how simple it all is, these toes
Playfully clutching the edge of a boulder.
It is a remote democracy, where men,
In manacles of place, outstare a sea
That rattles back its manacles of salt,
The moody jailer of the wild Atlantic.

    Traveller, tourist with your mind set on
Romantic Staffas and materials for
Winter conversations, if you should go there,
Landing at sunrise on its difficult shores,
On St Kilda you will surely hear Gaelic
Spoken softly like a poetry of ghosts
By those who never were contorted by
Hierarchies of cuisine and literacy.
You need only look at the faces of these men
Standing there like everybody's ancestors,
This flick of time I shuttered on a face.
Look at their sly, assuring mockery.
They are aware of what we are up to
With our internal explorations, our
Designs of affluence and education.
They know us so well, and are not jealous,
Whose be-all and end-all was an eternal
Casual husbandry upon a toehold

Of Europe, which, when failing, was not their fault.
You can see they have already prophesied
A day when survivors look across the stern
Of a departing vessel for the last time
At their gannet-shrouded cliffs, and the farewells
Of the St Kilda mouse and St Kilda wren
As they fall into the texts of specialists,
Ornithological visitors at the prow
Of a sullenly managed boat from the future.
They pose for ever outside their parliament,
Looking at me, as if they have grown from
Affection scattered across my own eyes.
And it is because of this that I, who took
This photograph in a year of many events –
The Zulu massacres, Tchaikovsky's opera –
Return to tell you this, and that after
My many photographs of distressed cities,
My portraits of successive elegants,
Of the emaciated dead, the lost empires,
Exploded fleets, and of the writhing flesh
Of dead civilians and commercial copulations,
That after so much of that larger franchise
It is to this island that I return.
Here I whittle time, like a dry stick,
From sunrise to sunset, among the groans
And sighings of a tongue I cannot speak,
Outside a parliament, looking at them,
As they, too, must always look at me
Looking through my apparatus at them
Looking. Benevolent, or malign? But who,
At this late stage, could tell, or think it worth it?
For I was there, and am, and I forget.

The Apple Tree

'And if the world should end tomorrow,
I still would plant my apple tree.'

Luther

I could play the bad eras like a concertina.
Multiple chords would squeak like 'excuse me',
'I beg your pardon', 'Oops' and 'Sorry, no thank you.'
Pump hard on a squeeze-box and you can almost hear
The Protestant clerks of northern Europe in Hell,
Complaisant men who filed the paperwork of death
Or signed the warrants, exemplary in private life
But puritanical before their desks of duty.
Say what you like, their Gods did not approve of them.

Men moaned of Scotland that its barren air and soil
Couldn't so much as ripen an apple. I can hear
Their croaked whispers reproach the stern and wild of Alba,
Naming our Kirk, our character, our coarse consent
To drunken decency and sober violence,
Our paradox of ways. Here, in the lovely land,
Beside Kirkmaiden, enumerating apple trees,
I feel the simple millions groan, 'Keep you your faith.
A sapling nursed to fruit impersonates salvation.'

Kirk-sanctioned crimes, Kirk-flourished trade, Kirk-coded
     commerce –
Say what you like, our Gods have not approved of them
While apples ripen round the mist-mild farms and gardens.
Good nature and a scent of fruit at dailygone
Make more of our acceptances and affirmations
Than quick links forced from character to climate.

Name you our beasts and trees, our rivers raced with fish,
Our islands, oceans, mountains and our field-sweet crops.
These too define a people named in city stone.

Four horses chew among the windfalls. Fallen fruits
Spill sweetening juices on the orchard grass, frosted
Into their leaking bruises and hoofed into pulp.
Last wasps grow fat and a tantrum of stings threatens
The man on his ladder, who cups an apple in
The stretch of his hand, then plucks it down, to bite
Its greeny red, rubbed on his overalls. He stands
Up there, eating an apple among all the apples
While big mares and their foals munch on the apple-grass.

At night the orchard is a brew of leaf and fruit,
Feeling the pinch of autumn. Spread sneddins release
The sounds that lie in wait in wood, and over there
An upland wilderness reposes in chilled beauty.
Burns spate with cleanliness of rain, that clean high ground
Of carrion crow and the left-alone mountain sheep.
Crag-country, wet and wiry, but fertile to the eye;
A lung-and-heart testing land, but by a ruin there
You will find crab-apple trees, black harp-strings in the
    wind.

Tonight I saw the stars trapped underneath the water.
I signed the simple covenant we keep with love.
One hand held out an apple while the other held
Earth from a kirkyard where the dead remember me.
In these lost hollows of the stern conventicles
A faith is kept with land and fruit. Already are
New scriptures written by the late-arriving autumn,
That postponed shuffle of leaves, that white frost-writing.
These are my missionary fruits, a kindred taste.

[73]

Then let my Gods be miracles brought on stone boats
By Conval and the first dailyday folk before him.
Rather an ordinary joy – a girl with a basket,
With apples under a linen cloth – than comfortless
With windlestrae to eat. Forge no false links of man
To land or creed, the true are good enough. Our lives
Crave codes of courtesy, ways of describing love,
And these, in a good-natured land, are ways to weep,
True comfort as you wipe your eyes and try to live.

An Address on the Destitution of Scotland

Who would have thought it, and not me, not me,
That a boy who shawed turnips with a large gully
By the side of Cousar's cart and snort-breathed Clydesdale,
Who worked in the blue-and-red darkening dusk of
    childhood,
Would grow into this archivist of Red desires?
Far away are the chills of original Octobers.
My eyes are heavy now with alien perspectives,
And I am sick of the decisions of philosophers –
Dirty hands, dirty hands of turncoats and opinion-makers.
It was a long road back to this undeclared Republic.
I came by the by-ways, empty of milestones,
On the roads of old drovers, by disused workings.

So here I am, returned to your shabby encampments.
I, too, have scrounged on open fields, ripped up
Into their gathering of released good stinks
That mingle in the first-few-hours-of-shaws-rotting,
That reek of roots, that tactile, lunatic aroma
Tasting of dialect and curses sent out to work.

Tell me of your tinkerdom, of this poverty
Among you, raddled by a destitute polity,
The fields abandoned to old supermarket trolleys,
An ancient soot, the Clyde returning to its nature.
On which blasphemy do you blame your outcast silence,
Bedraggled here with your billy-cans and supper?

Share with me, then, the sad glugs in your bottles;
Throw a stolen spud for me on the side-embers.
Allow me to pull up a brick, and to sit beside you
In this nocturne of modernity, to speak of the dead,
Of the creatures loping from their dens of extinction.
Who are you waiting for? The stern mountain-preacher
In his coat of biblical night? I have seen him.
He sleeps in a kiln, out of the way of dragoons;
And I met a subversive optimist, at Sanquhar.
Permit me, then, to join your circle around your fire
In this midden of warm faces and freezing backs.
Sing me your songs in the speech of timber and horse.

Dominies

White is the January, and schoolboys' scuffed
Footprints in the snow lead to the sound of a bell.
It is Scotland and I attend the dead dominies.
A hand is spinning the globe, saying 'Galileo'
In a cold classroom, in a puff of chalk-dust.
Dominies, dead now, forgive these gauche lines,
My compromised parsings. Boyhood's grammarians
Set down the long examination, 'ink exercises'
At moments of mania, running riot through
The iron language like a trill of angry Rs.

[75]

'What sorts of men were the Caesars? Did you heave an axe,
At the wall, against them? Did you stand for your country?
Keep up with the translation. It is good for you.
Horace. Livy. Ballantyne. I am already historical.'

Witch-girl

For ever more, they said, that girl was lame
In hands and feet, and that, they said, was proof
The lightless Devil spelled her into horse,
Moulding her hands and feet in solid hoof.

Poor girl, her mother saddled her, then rode
Through Sutherland until the outraged Law
Attended to the giddy-ups of gossip,
Force-feeding both of them on Tolbooth straw.

Only her mother was condemned. A pious mob –
Citizens and presbyters – whinnied, neighed,
Clip-clopped, as, standing in their fear of God,
There too were men who watched but also pitied.

Cold day in Dornoch ... Shivering, the witch
Relieved her freezing round that fire which burned
To burn her up. Crowds psalmed with horror.
She blistered in the tar and, screaming, burned.

They spoke in Dornoch how the horses mourned
And how that lame girl, wandering, was heard
Tearing at the grass; and how she sat and sang,
As if the Devil also made her bird;

And how she washed her lameness in the rivers
From Oykell to the Clyde and Tweed and Forth,
Notorious as something to be pitied,
A girl to look at but a beast in worth.

No one could see her but would think he saw
Hoof in her fumbling hands, her staggering gait.
They spurned her flowers, as if they'd grown from her;
They barbed their righteous charity with hate.

She hawked her flowers in Glasgow, by the Trongate;
In Edinburgh, selling flowers, she slept
Beside the braziers of the City Guard.
The earth and animals within her wept.

No one to help her; no one saw her die,
If she is dead. By Gryfe, by Deveron,
By Cree and Tay, I see her wash her lameness,
And hear her breathing in the wood and stone.

Washing the Coins

You'd start at seven, and then you'd bend your back
Until they let you stand up straight, your hands
Pressed on your kidneys as you groaned for lunch,
Thick sandwiches in grease-proofed bundles, piled
Beside the jackets by the hawthorn hedges.
And then you'd bend your little back again
Until they let you stand up straight. Your hands,
On which the earth had dried in layers, itched, itched,
Though worse still was that ache along the tips
Of every picking finger, each broken nail
That scraped the ground for sprawled potatoes

The turning digger churned out of the drills.
Muttering strong Irish men and women worked
Quicker than local boys. You had to watch them.
They had the trick of sideways-bolted spuds
Fast to your ear, and the upset wire basket
That broke your heart but made the Irish laugh.
You moaned, complained, and learned the rules of work.
Your boots, enlarging as the day wore on,
Were weighted by the magnets of the earth,
And rain in the face was also to have
Something in common with bedraggled Irish.
You held your hands into the rain, then watched
Brown water drip along your chilling fingers
Until you saw the colour of your skin
Through rips disfiguring your gloves of mud.
It was the same for everyone. All day
That bead of sweat tickled your smeared nose
And a glance upwards would show you trees and clouds
In turbulent collusions of the sky
With ground and ground with sky, and you portrayed
Among the wretched of the native earth.
Towards the end you felt you understood
The happy rancour of the Irish howkers.
When dusk came down, you stood beside the byre
For the farmer's wife to pay the labour off.
And this is what I remember by the dark
Whitewash of the byre wall among shuffling boots.
She knew me, but she couldn't tell my face
From an Irish boy's, and she apologized
And roughed my hair as into my cupped hands
She poured a dozen pennies of the realm
And placed two florins there, then cupped her hands
Around my hands, like praying together.

It is not good to feel you have no future.
My clotted hands turned coins to muddy copper.
I tumbled all my coins upon our table.
My mother ran a basin of hot water.
We bathed my wages and we scrubbed them clean.
Once all that sediment was washed away,
That residue of field caked on my money,
I filled the basin to its brim with cold;
And when the water settled I could see
Two English kings among their drowned Britannias.

Galloway Motor Farm

They spoil a farm, already written off
Against experience or income tax –
Two Land Rovers, several tractors,
These wooden cattle-floats like shanty huts;
A Jaguar, garaged in the air and grass,
On highways of self-heal and lady's bedstraw;
A Morris shooting-brake is bedded down
With agricultural gear and tackle.

Scattered beside derelict byres and barns,
Awkward, out of place, they lie here, eyesores
Cast out from progress, maladroitly banned
Machinery, discarded implements.
Wastrel existences, I can hear them
As each one wrestles free of function,
Picked over, plundered by who dumped them here,
Already scavenged for their feus of scrap.

The chemistry of weather has installed
Its scaffolding, from which it builds its rusts
On the iron of a horse-drawn reaper.
Air braces itself before stinging nettles.
Car doors, bumpers, bonnets, mudguards, engines –
Earth will not have them back until their steels,
Their chromes, veneers and leathers marry with
These stony contours as the brides of place.

I will be glad to have been here, living
Within this stung bubble where antiquities
Freshen, where they breathe the present tense.
Docken, yarrow, the muscular turf, ignore
These rubbished profits and spent wages.
It all means less than nothing to the bat
On his manic itinerary, and the fox
Was born too late to live with other landmarks.

As for a man, then he may walk beside
These thumbed-down vehicles, posing the moon
Against the window of a truck's high cabin;
Or sit inside, behind the wheel, thinking
A roadless countryside as he pretends
He's motoring through the night. Scotland, come back
From the lost ground of your dismantled lands.
A carelessness has defaced even the bluebell.

Tonight, by a steading, an iron reaper
That once outscythed the scythe
Is a silent cry of its materials,
With all its blunt blades yearning for the stone.
It has come from the yonside of invention,
From pulverable ore and foundry hammers.
Old harness rots above the rusted horseshoes.
Unborn horses graze on the back pastures.

Monumental Sculptor

That look on his face, consulting
His telephone directory,
Is a respectful smirk,
A shading of his dusty eyebrows.

Stooped round his left-hand grip
On a chisel, he is there to tell us
His hammered catalogue of names
Is the stone book of his town.

With lean, ridged muscles of
A man who works with stone,
He sculpts his alphabets
Of memory and consolation.

Notice the slow certainty
Of how his two apprentices
Come round to his likeness,
Inheriting his cut languages.

In the hut of his office
Are spiked invoices and a Bible.
He is in the fashion of God
In that black jacket he wears

When his customers call,
Holding his price-lists and designs,
Discussing the choice of words.
A kettle boils among the stone-dust.

I hear his phone ringing,
As, with a genuflecting crane,
Which squeaks of chains, of stretched links,
They hoist a finished page of marble.

There is no need to answer it,
Not in this trade. The name
Will still be there tomorrow
For his craft of the Kirk's loved ones.

The Harp of Renfrewshire
Contemplating a map

Annals of the trilled R, gently stroked L,
Lamenting O of local literature,
Open, on this, their one-page book, a still
Land-language chattered in a river's burr.

Small-talk of herdsmen, rural argument –
These soft disputes drift over river-meadows,
A darg of conversations, a verbal scent –
Tut-tutted discourse, time of day, word-brose.

Named places have been dictionaried in
Ground's secret lexicon, its racial moan
Of etymology and cries of pain
That slit a summer wind and then were gone.

A mother calls her daughter from her door.
Her house, my stone illusion, hugs its hill.
From Eaglesham west to the rocky shore
Her cry is stretched across bog-asphodel.

The patronymic miles of grass and weddings,
Their festivals of gender, covenants,
Poor pre-industrially scattered steadings,
Ploughed-up davochs – old names, inhabitants.

And on my map is neither wall or fence,
But men and women and their revenue,
As, watching them, I utter into silence
A granary of whispers rinsed in dew.

War Blinded

For more than sixty years he has been blind
Behind that wall, these trees, with terrible
Longevity wheeled in the sun and wind
On pathways of the soldiers' hospital.

For half that time his story's troubled me –
That showroom by the ferry, where I saw
His basketwork, a touch-turned filigree
His fingers coaxed from charitable straw;

Or how he felt when young, enlisting at
Recruiting tables on the football pitch,
To end up slumped across a parapet,
His eye-blood running in a molten ditch;

Or how the light looked when I saw two men,
One blind, one in a wheelchair, in that park,
Their dignity, which I have not forgotten,
Which helps me struggle with this lesser dark.

That war's too old for me to understand
How he might think, nursed now in wards of want,
Remembering that day when his right hand
Gripped on the shoulder of the man in front.

Savings

She saved her money
And she hid her money in
An oriental tin
That came from Twining's Tea.
– 'Oh, how much money have you now?'
But she'd never let me see.
She'd place that tin into my hands,
Then with her hands on mine
She'd help me shake her Twining's tin –
Half-crowns and a sovereign,
Shillings, sixpences and florins
Rattled on the paper notes.
That was her funeral fund
I was too young to understand.
When I did, and she was dead,
It wasn't death that I could see
In tea-leaves sifting from a spoon
That came out of a Chinese tin.
I saw the life she'd shovelled in.

Rose

So, little rose, it is all over
And you need no longer
Explore your cupped shapes,
Your fine organic enamels.

Four days you sat there
In a simple blue glass.
I watched you, I watched you;
I kept my eye on you.

My love is four days gone from me.
You have been good company.
I knew it would be like this –
You'd die the day of her return.

You have sat there in silence
Like a thought prayer.
You have been my good intentions.
You listened to me with patience.

Now I am in a gentle panic,
Not knowing what to do with you.
I will make up a ritual
For the departures of roses.

You will go into the heaven
Of unforgotten things.
Matisse will paint you;
Or Samuel Peploe will.

The door of her taxi is closing.
But you did not tell me your secrets.
I shall drink the water
Which did not preserve you long enough.

I will remember you in the French language.
I eat you now to keep you for ever.
Hello, my love. See?
This thorn has cut my lips.

Saturday

For Sandra and Chetwyn

Driving along the B1248
We pass such villages as Wetwang, or
North Grimston of descending Z-bends.
The Wolds are rolling for our benefit;
The long woods stride towards the eastern shore.
Frost sparks refrigerated ploughland to
A fan of silver ribs, good husbandry
In straight lines, going downhill to a point,
A misted earthen star, half-frost, half-ground.
And we are going to our country friends
At Kirkbymoorside, bearing a pineapple,
Some books of interest and a fine Bordeaux.
I wish it to be today, always, one hour
On this, the pleasant side of history.

Courting

On a summer's night to come
We'll find ourselves walking
Through a familiar Park.
I feel it happening –
Surprised anachronisms
In a delight, posed as
Hand-holding listeners to
Light overtures, percussed
From a lanterned bandstand
Through shaken foliage.

An autumn afternoon
Rehearses mist and brown
For a rediscovery –
That colour of angels
Flighted with chestnut leaves
Above the arrogant
Scarf-tightening waterfall,
A down-roar of water
Into the sinister
Conventional shadows.

It is already chosen,
A retrospective Sunday
When the still lake is glazed,
When bird-bread breaks underfoot,
Frost-toasted on cinder paths
And rhododendrons look
Snowed green exotica,
A botany of drips:
We will walk there again
With our white conversations.

Gardened from countryside,
The Park heaps love-days
On nature's edge; it is
An album of the Spring
In that season: woodland's
Municipal surprise,
Vernal formalities,
Mute orchestras of bluebells
When light leans on the leaf
And the thrush sings of rain.

Come with me now, dear girl,
And we will walk our years
Together. They open,
As gates do, or books, the heart's
Preliminary landmarks –
That path that leads nowhere
And a meadow beyond;
This path that leads into
Wilder greens of love,
A grass for walking on.

E. A. Walton Thinks of Painting 'The Daydream'

I kissed my sweet girl-cousins
One by one
Then they grew up
And I never saw them again.
They are lost among
Marriages and houses
At places where
Farms run out of fields
And towns begin.
I remember a girl
Who looked at her own future,
Lying among the flowers –
Milk-pail and butter-churn,
A belled cow led home
On a frayed halter.

The Local

Come, let us lower the tone, talking in
These smoky cadences and lounge-bar whispers.
We will enumerate the lost realia.
The Spirit of the Age will turn its back
And run away from such a narrative.
Notice how beer-mats slip a little on
These inconspicuous pools of slop and spillage.
It suggests half an epiphany is happening.
Or what else is it, tilting in my head,
Which makes me watch the sandwiches grow stale,
That slow bending of bread in perspex bins
At the end of the bar? That, too, explains
A revolution or a crazed malaise
In the wink of a listening stranger.
I can hear music in the oiled hinges
When that door opens, a memory of
Unwritten Mozart or a lost Haydn
In the old man whistling in the Gents
Among the cisterns. Matisse emerges from
A doodled beer-mat; a fingernail engraves
An odalisque from a remembered girl
In a wet bar-counter's puddled drainage.
A man stands muttering his faulty tales
Of Burma in the last days of its Raj.
His eyes glint like a kukri in his dark
Leaf-hidden forays. 'Arakan,' he says,
To no one. 'Rajput. Frightened. Subahdar.'
The Empire ends here, in his anecdotes.
Now add to this the humming of an unplayed
Juke-box. Add chattering at corner tables.
You can hear what I mean in the whirred blades

Of the ventilator's recitations.
Its draughty epic is a literature
Depicting murky ale and tragic drunks
Who were lovers and heroes once, in days
No longer as these ones we live now among
Susurrations and vague moral endeavour.
I shall ingratiate myself with God,
Sticking it out in the land of the living.
Placebo Domino in regione vivorum.
The juke-box hammers out its antiphon.
They service it by feeding in new anthems.
And someone sings, a would-be dandy with
A withered buttonhole. My brain opens.
The streets are bathed in summer and a man
Who's five pence short of what a refill costs
Rejects the dandy's overstated affluence.
We could commune with our ancestors,
Whoever they were. We could talk of life
And death and poetry. We could be neutral,
Smiling with goodwill. Instead, we stand
In this armpit of English vernacular,
Hopelessly in touch with where we are.
The dead lie under our feet like pipelines.
The unacknowledged, counting pennies from
An outstretched palm, know what compassion's worth,
Here, humbly, off a High Street in the North.

Remembering Lunch

Noticing from what they talk about, and how they stand, or
    walk,
That my friends have lost the ability or inclination to wander
Along the shores of an estuary or sea in contented solitude,
Disturbs me on the increasingly tedious subject of myself.
I long for more chances to walk along depopulated shores,
For more hours dedicated to fine discriminations of mud
As it shades from grey to silver or dries into soft pottery;
Discriminations of wind, sky, rough grasses and water-birds,
And, above all, to be well-dressed in tweeds and serviceable
    shoes
Although not like an inverted popinjay of the demented
    gentry
But as a schoolmaster of some reading and sensibility
Circa 1930 and up to his eccentric week-end pursuits,
    noticing,
Before the flood of specialists, the trace of lost peoples
In a partly eroded mound, marks in the earth, or this and
    that
Turned over with the aforementioned impermeable
    footwear.
Describing this to my strangely sophisticated companions
Is to observe them docket it for future reference in
A pigeon-hole of the mind labelled Possible Satires.
We are far gone in our own decay. I admit it freely,
Longing no more for even the wherewithal of decent
    sufficiency
Or whatever hypothetical brilliance makes it possible.
Whatever my friends long for, they no longer confess it
In the afternoon twilight of a long lunch in London
After that moment when the last carafe has been ordered.

Such delicate conversations of years gone by! You would think
Perceptions of this sort best left for approaching senility,
Especially as, in my case, I was not born ever to expect
To enjoy so long-drawn-out a lunchtime at steep prices
Among tolerant waiters resigned to our lasting presences
As if they sense a recapitulation by young men of young men
In that fine hour of Edwardian promise at the *Tour Eiffel*
Or expatriate Americans and Irishmen in 'twenties Paris.
It is pretty well standard among literary phenomena.
Whether in the Rome of Marcus Martialis or London ordinaries
Favoured by roaring playwrights and poets destined for
Future righteousness or a destructive addiction to sack,
Lunch, lunch is a unitary principle, as Balzac would tell you
And as any man of letters consulting his watch towards noon
Would undoubtedly endorse. Lunch is the business of capitals,
Whether in *L'Escargot Bienvenue, Gobbles*, or the cheap Italian joint.
Impoverished or priggish in the provinces, where talent is born,
The angry poets look towards London as to a sea of restaurants,
Cursing the overpriced establishments of where they live
And the small scatter of the like-minded not on speaking terms.
But even this pleasure has waned, and its sum of parts –
People shaking hands on the pavement, a couple entering
A taxi hailed in the London rain, the red tears on a bottle
And the absorbing conspiracies and asserted judgements
Of young men in the self-confident flush of their promise –
Its sum of parts no longer presents a street of epiphanies.

Too much now has been spoken, or published, or
    unpublished.
Manias without charm, cynicism without wit, and integrity
Lying around so long it has begun to stink, can be seen and
    heard.
To come down south from the country in a freshly pressed
    suit
Is no longer the exercise in youthful if gauche dignity
It was once in days of innocent enthusiasm without routine.
And so I look forward to my tweed-clad solitude, alone
Beside a widening estuary, the lighthoused island appearing
Where waves of the sea turmoil against the river's waters
Baring their salty teeth and roaring. And here I can stand –
Forgive me my fantasies as, Lord, I surely forgive you
    yours –
In a pretence of being a John Buchan of the underdog,
With my waistcoated breast puffed against the wind. What
    do they long for?
Propping up bars with them I can pretend to be as they are
Though I no longer know what they are thinking, if ever I
    did,
And, raising this civil if not entirely sympathetic interest
In what they feel, I know it contributes little to them,
Adding, as it does, to a change in myself they might not
    notice,
Causing me this pain as I realize the way I must change
Is to be different from friends I love and whose company –
When the last carafe was ordered, an outrageous remark
    spoken,
Or someone announced his plan for an innovating stanza
Or a new development in his crowded sex-life – whose
    company
Was a landmark in my paltry accumulation of knowledge.

Perhaps, after all, this not altogether satisfactory
Independence of mind and identity before larger notions
Is a better mess to be in, with a pocketful of bread and
    cheese,
My hipflask and the *Poésie* of Philippe Jaccottet,
Listening to the sea compose its urbane wilderness,
Although it is a cause for fear to notice that only my
    footprints
Litter this deserted beach with signs of human approach,
Each squelch of leather on mud complaining, *But where are
    you going?*

Green Breeks

J. G. Lockhart, *Memoirs of Sir Walter Scott*,
Macmillan, 1900, Vol. 1, pages 81–5.

Crosscauseway, Bristo Street, and Potterrow,
In Edinburgh, seventeen eighty-three –
    Boys there were poor, their social class was 'low';
    Their futures lay in work or livery.
Sir Walter Scott says they 'inhabited'
These streets they lived on; but, in George's Square,
    'The author's father' – so Sir Walter said –
    Did not 'inhabit' but 'resided' there.
Young Walter and his chums were organized
Into a 'company' or 'regiment'.
    A 'lady of distinction', who despised
    The ragged street-boys from the tenements,
Gave Scott 'a handsome set of colours', which
Made Walter grateful to that Highland bitch
Who'd later 'clear' her kinsmen from her land,
That Duchess-Countess named for Sutherland.

From Potterrow, Crosscauseway, Bristo Street,
The poor boys came to 'bicker' on the Square –
    A military game, if indiscreet –
    To thrash the sons of those 'residing' there.
Offspring of State, Law, Ministry and Bank,
With flag aloft, defended their regime
    Against those 'chiefly of the lower rank',
    Boy-battles at a simplified extreme.
Though vanquished from the subtly written book
That's history, the street-boys often won –
    Scott says they did. Sir Walter undertook
    Average lies in how he wrote it down –
Mendacious annals – that no one should forget
When beggars win, they're in the horsemen's debt;
And only Scott has chronicled their war –
A beaten boy becomes the conqueror.

One of his enemies, says Scott, was both
Ajax and Achilles of the Crosscauseway –
    'The very picture of a youthful Goth' –
    The first to fight and last to run away.
Blue-eyed, with long fair hair, tall, finely made,
That boy-barbarian awed him. Scott could tell
    He and his class-mates mustered to degrade
    This brave, presumptious, vulgar general.
They called him Green Breeks, this boy whom Scott preserved
As a memento of his opposite
    That, cheating him of what he led and served,
    A novelist could have his way with it.
Scott draws the colour of his hero's eyes,
His shape, his height, but not the boy, who dies
Within the pickle of Scott's quickened prose,
Half-loved by Scott, half-feared, born to oppose.

In one fight, Green Breeks laid his hands upon
Sutherland's 'patrician standard'. Before
        He'd time to win it, he was faced with one
        Too zealous for 'the honour of the Corps'
Who had a hanger or *couteau de chasse*.
For honour, then, that boy cut Green Breeks down.
        To save a flag, the honour of his class,
        He struck him on the head and cut him down.
Imagined horsemen of the old regime
Transformed young Green Breeks to a Dying Gaul –
        A pictured history, the bronze of dream,
        A classic gesture in an urban brawl.
Scott's friend disgraced his 'regiment' and showed
Expedient dragoonship was its code.
Where was nobility? But Scott, you found
Your life's obsession on that cobbled ground.

Scott turned our country round upon its name
And time. Its history obeyed his whip
        When Scott sent out his characters to claim
        Their pedigrees in Green Breeks' leadership.
I do not understand, Scott, what you meant
By your displaced verse-prose 'nobility'
        Unless the tatters of your 'regiment'
        Were patched on Green Breeks, that, for chivalry,
Your heroes might go forth and look the part –
Part man, part prince, part soldier and part God –
        Ridiculous and lacking in support
        As, when they fall, mere modern men applaud.
But Scott, you failed; for where your Green Breeks lives
Is that dark tenement of fugitives
Who, fled from time, have no need to endure
The quicklime of your ordered literature.

Green Breeks did not inform. He kept his pride.
He nursed his lovely grudge and sword-cracked skull
 And took both pain and bribery in his stride.
 They offered cash, 'smart money', to annul
Shame and dishonoured laws. He would not sell
His wound: let them remember it. Scott says
 That childish purse was small – part comical,
 Part serious: the whole antithesis.
They would not meet him face to face, but stood
On dignity and used a go-between,
 Like states, transacting with the multitude,
 Who can negotiate, then intervene
With laws, with cavalry and troops, with style,
With system, representatives and guile,
Who, pompously, can compromise to win,
Pitch coins against a ragged ostentation.

Peasant baroque, like this, its nuts screwed tight
In praise of rabbles and those *sans culottes*,
 Won't change a thing. It whets an appetite,
 Unfankling truths inwoven like a knot.
It gestures like a ghost towards a ghost,
And, bringing Green Breeks back, or trying to,
 It reckons with desire, the human cost
 In losing what was old, and fierce, and true.
What did he do? Where did he live, and die?
That life can be imagined. I let him *be*.
 He is my light, conspirator and spy.
 He is perpetual. He is my country.
He is my people's minds, when they perceive
A native truth persisting in the weave
Of shabby happenings. When they turn their cheeks
The other way, he turns them back, my Green Breeks.

Green Breeks accepted what he asked them give –
A pound of snuff for 'some old woman – aunt,
       Grandmother, or the like,' with whom he lived.
       Kindness, like courtesy, must ever haunt
Love-raddled reminiscence, Walter Scott.
You cannot hide behind mock-epic prose
       Your love of 'haves', amusement at 'have-nots'.
       Between your lines, it's easy to suppose
Deeper affections generate each word
Recalling Green Breeks in your years of fame.
       You drank toasts to his name in Abbotsford,
       Proposed to Green Breeks, not his father's name.
Be not amused, Scott. Go, and give him thanks
He let you patronize his 'lower ranks'.
Go, talk to him, and tell him who you are,
Face to face, at last, Scott; and kiss his scar.

Tannahill
Robert Tannahill, 1774–1810

'I would I were a weaver, I could sing all manner of songs.'
                                                    Shakespeare

       Aye, Bobbie Tannahill, I'll brew
       Unhappy truths of verse and you
       In Scots lines of the turn and screw.
              Aye, Tannahill,
       This reckoning is overdue,
              Lamentable.

We sang your songs in Paisley's school,
Ink-fingered Dux and classroom fool,
Each little lord of ridicule;
  Aye, Tannahill,
All learned your sweet and bountiful
  Melodic drill.

By singing you, I understood
That poetry's lax brotherhood
Lived in my town; and it was good –
  Aye, Tannahill –
To learn that verse did not exclude
  A local skill.

Blackboyds and yeltrins in the year
Seventeen hundred and seventy-four
Were ripe and brilliant, born to dare
  'The sin of rhyme'
That Burns committed in his pure
  Intimate crime.

In seventeen hundred and eighty-six
They set you learn a weaver's tricks
While Burns discovered Muses vex
  As well as grace,
Young Burns, whose Scots proprietrix
  Spat in his face.

Douce dandies of the posh salons
Took that man in, as if on loan,
Then having raised, they laid him down,
  Their ploughman poet.
They made Society's decision,
  And let him know it.

Burns, Tannahill and Fergusson,
These jorum-jirgers, they could hone
A merry R, lick till they shone
    Gently stroked Ls,
And then die young, or in Darien,
    Ink's asphodels.

Young dead like Leyden, Smith and Gray,
Unread, forgotten, sternly weigh
Against the doors of elegy
    And find them shut.
Timor mortis conturbat me –
    Not to forget.

An antiquarian of old airs,
You played your flute at Renfrew's fairs;
You sang of amorous despairs
    And country courting.
Aye, Tannahill, hurt love confers
    A sweeter singing.

Composing verses at your bench,
Lines woven inch by linen inch
To follow each iambic hunch
    Into its art,
You sang, like a beginning finch,
    Your common heart.

A wabster's craft would teach a man
To live with art as an artisan.
As you could weave, teach me to scan
    And turn a rhyme,
Fraternally, like Caliban
    His low sublime.

When Paisley's bodies sought to learn
At the Star Inn and the Sun Tavern,
You, Tannahill, taught them discern
        False verse from true.
They 'kenned y'r faither', and would turn
        Their wits on you.

Once set in print, that was enough;
Your melodies had had their puff,
Their papery chance. With each rebuff
        Your inkwells dried;
You, Tannahill, in local chaff,
        Were vilified.

My Tannahill, the delicate
Delight of poetry is to wait
And, suffering the alphabet,
        Allow songs come
The way a prodigal in debt
        Walks slowly home.

You could not wait, yet overheard
A fame that rarely is conferred –
Anonymously choristered,
        A song you wrote;
A farm-girl, singing as she sheared,
        Your song, her throat.

And still they are singing, by Gryfe,
By Cart, with gentle disbelief
In the lilt of words against life;
        And your words breathe
In the pianos, with a little laugh,
        Keeping their faith.

Gone, gone down, with a song, gone down,
My Tannahill. The tavern town
Said one book was your last and frowned.
        The River Cart
Ran deep and waste where you would drown,
        Your counterpart.

You clutched the papers of your tongue:
Gone, gone down, gone down with a song.
Pity the mad, darkened with wrong.
        Home Lycidas,
You died in the dish-cloth Cart, among
        The ugliness.

And in the morning schoolboys came
To fish for papers, speak your name
And take their landed catches home,
        Dried on the gorse;
Aye, Tannahill, boys caught your poems,
        Lost, watery verse.

By broom, by briar, by Craigie Wood,
Through Cart-side's river neighbourhood,
Your papers rotting on the mud,
        My Tannahill!
But the shelfie and the hawthorn bud
        You could not kill.

The Gallery

See, how this lady rises on her swing
Encouraged by the brush of Fragonard,
As light as love, as ruthless as the Czar,
Who, from her height, looks down on everything.

When on a canvas an oil-eye of blue
Has tiny fissures, you can stand behind,
Imagine time, observe, and condescend,
Wink at and spit on those who are not you.

Out of the eye of Christ, you might see God;
Or, from your swing, see pastoral machines
Romanticized, re-made as guillotines;
Or, Goya's captive, face a firing-squad;

Or, Goya's soldier, be condemned to hear
Eternity in the museum of death –
Your moment after triggering – and with
The horror of aesthetics in your ears.

Ah, they were lucky, who were drawn from life
By river-banks in summer, in café scenes,
The way they were, for all their speechless pains,
That absinthe drinker and his sober wife.

The Deserter
Homage to Robert Desnos

'Somewhere in the world, at the foot of an embankment,
A deserter parleys with sentries who don't understand his
*   language.'*

At the world's end, just before everything stops,
There may not be a war going on, but it is where
Broken lines of contested frontiers converge,
Drawn long ago by the hands of shrewd statesmen
In the years when they bagged the knees and elbows of their
    suits
In the grandest of all the world's capital cities.

It is at this place they keep the railway carriages
Of armistice and treaties, those waggons which brought
The revolutionary and his bales of pamphlets.
Many cattle trucks rot on a spread of sidings
With their memories of last kisses, of goodbyes,
A child's hand in yours, his eyes under the skip of his cap.

This is the last mortuary, the bottom inch of six feet,
Home to pallid garrisons sustained on cigarettes
And fantasies of strangers, wrapped in greatcoats
The way the inflexible uphold their ideologies.
Their freezing breath fastens them as if by chains
To a heaven above the arc-lamps, above innocent airliners.

Snow has begun to fall on the guilty secrets of Europe.
Here, where the lines meet, and emplacements rise up
Out of mined earth in their laurels of wire, a man,
Unarmed, talks with another five who hold their guns
On him. This conversation is composed of cloth,
Of buttons, stars, and boots. Of wood. Of steel. Of wire.

'A spectre in a well-tailored shroud
Smoked a cigar at the window of his apartment.'

We have seen him, this upright father
Who has the stately manners of a priest,
Who, when he lets it slip, behaves like a tycoon
In armaments, believing that they died
In Buchenwald for capitalism, for him.

We have dined with this stranger, talked at meat
With him after the funerals of our fathers.
Our wives are fond of him. They have been known to
Abscond to some Swiss chalet with him where
He keeps the instruments of pleasure.

How confidently the ash balances on
The tip of his cigar, a grey drool;
And with what contempt for his possessions
He lets it fall ... We have seen him in cafés,
Served, as if he has only to wave his hand.

We are asked to die for him, and we die.
In the unlikeliest places, we have died,
Places we never dreamt of sending postcards from.
There, in his red resorts, men vanish in
Factories that grind through men and native parishes.

Never to die, not even in the grand style
Tended by nieces married to Counts and Princes,
But to live always, at the concept of wealth,
In galleries and in the regularity of verse,
In metronomes pledged to custom,

And in the regulation of wages and bread,
Never to die. O with how much passion
We can condemn this man many have died for.
He claims even to love nature.
He praises its brutality as he hunts.

In his mouth is the taste of Europe,
Its rank saliva. When I see this ghost,
I am afraid of him, who, from his window,
Spits on the lives of so many people,
On my mother, my father, my wife, my friends, myself.

'A widow in her wedding-grown gets into the wrong train.'

So much is average, so much
That anyone can buy or touch,
Things you can watch, or put to sleep,
That walk, or run on wheels, or creep.

Other things are just mistaken,
Marriages, or wrong trains taken.
A widow in her wedding-gown
Alights somewhere, in the wrong town.

O Lady, run, it's over now,
Whatever grief that marked your brow
With something like a brilliant star
To tell this city who you are.

I shall possess your soul, bereaved
Of everything for which it lived.
I am a specialist of tears.
I weep the world's, let me weep yours.

I listen to the song you sing
About two lives, two wedding-rings.
I listen as you fold your dress
To the mute curves of your nakedness.

Lamp-posts

You find them in the cities of Europe,
Ornate plush iron, stooped, fluted, winged,
And in the postures of old *boulevardiers*.
They stand outside hotels and embassies
As the commissionaires of *savoir faire*
And architecture, dressed in an era
Along the fashionable avenues.
In Paris like the ghosts of Baudelaire,
And in Prague like a street of Kafkas,
They contemplate the shadows round their feet.
Throw them a coin or two, for they are beggars
Touting beneath electric epaulettes
For the recovery of time, for hooves,
For carriages and footmen, or for her
Habsburgian slipper fallen in a pulse
Of gas-light and an equerry kneeling
To fit the slipper to its royal foot.
The rehabilitated lamps of Warsaw
Have been hung with civilians, improvised
As gallows while the multitudes of death
Marched over the rubble, in the darkness.
Therefore I mourn these uprooted lamp-posts
That lean against a wall, in a corner of

This warehouse, bleak, municipal, leaning
In stances of exhaustion, their arms across
Their eyes, their brows against a bare brick wall.

Loch Music

I listen as recorded Bach
Restates the rhythms of a loch.
Through blends of dusk and dragonflies
A music settles on my eyes
Until I hear the living moors,
Sunk stones and shadowed conifers,
And what I hear is what I see,
A summer night's divinity.
And I am not administered
Tonight, but feel my life transferred
Beyond the realm of where I am
Into a personal extreme,
As on my wrist, my eager pulse
Counts out the blood of someone else.
Mist-moving trees proclaim a sense
Of sight without intelligence;
The intellects of water teach
A truth that's physical and rich.
I nourish nothing with the stars,
With minerals, as I disperse,
A scattering of quavered wash
As light against the wind as ash.

Ode to a Paperclip

When I speak to you, paperclip, urging you
To get a move on and metamorphose,
You sit there mating with the light that shines
Out of your minerals, a brighter glint
Where, rounding at a loop, you meet the sun.
Paperclip, I like you, I need you.
Please, turn into something wonderful.

   I remember restless clerks, in boring places,
Unbend you to caress their ears, tickling
Their lobes, or, slowly, linking you until
They forged one of their office necklaces –
A daisy-chain, from flowers of the desk;
Or straighten you, to dab at inky fluff
Mossed round a comma or an asterisk.

   You have more uses than your name pretends.
Intimately fingered all late afternoon,
Frustrations weave you into metal knots,
Boredom's insignia in the typing-pools.
A secretary, composed but fidgeting,
Was once chastised with airborne paperclips,
But no one noticed what was being thrown.

   A box of you, when brought up from the store,
Then opened, looked at, looks like dying sprats,
All life in its pathetic multiples.
But these are not your proper transformations.
Who knows what purpose you'll be made to serve
When a suspender is in deep crisis, or
The manager's braces tear his buttons off?

   It's you they think of first, because they know
Your versatility can be delivered
On bodice straps or snapped elastics.

It's your neutrality that gets me down –
Disarming. Why do you do it? You work
On dictats to the underlings of death
As readily as you fasten up the drafts
  A democrat compiles on human rights.
Good and/or bad, important/unimportant –
Little survivor, you go where you're sent,
On memoranda from the Chiefs of Staff
To Ministers of State, down to the note
A man finds clipped inside his wage packet,
Saying, *Sorry, you've been made redundant.*
  You also get lost and nobody cares.
It's part of your status to turn up in
A handful of change, or to appear from
Her handbag when she's powdering her nose.
You've no prestige at all, a tiny one
Among the commonplace, the vacuumed millions,
Diminished things, the meek disposables.
  Hand-made gold-plated paperclips do not,
I am sure of it, get made, let alone
Presented at executive goodbyes,
Although I've seen a breasty typist wear you
As earrings and, on her, you looked like treasure.
More than familiars, more than desk-top trinkets,
You're precious, though we may not choose to say so.
  Give them gold watches or cut-glass decanters,
It's you they're likely to remember as
The days go by, watched from their patios,
As, too, they think of Miss-What-Was-Her-Name –
Evasive, leggy and impertinent –
The one who worked gymnastic, sculptural
Designs in wire, her secretarial art.
  Ubiquitous, docile and mass-produced,

Existing in relationship to work
And tedium expressed thereof, you are
As functional as roads or pen and ink.
A box of you, when shaken on the ear,
Can make Brazilian noises, a rhythmic sea,
Plural as salt, as leaves, as citizens.
   Ghost-bullets, triple-loops, no matter what
Inquiring minds might call your outline capsules,
You change your shapes and will go anywhere,
Do anything for a piece of the action.
Immoralist! Turncoat! Mercenary!
You don't need her, or him – Love me; love me,
And go where I go, gentle talisman.

Ratatouille

I

Consider, please, this dish of ratatouille.
Neither will it invade Afghanistan
Or boycott the Olympic Games in a huff.
It likes the paintings of Raoul Dufy.
It feeds the playboy and the working-man.
Of wine and sun it cannot get enough.
It has no enemies, no, not even
Salade niçoise or phoney recipes,
Not Leonid Brezhnev, no, not Ronald Reagan.
It is the fruits of earth, this ratatouille,
And it has many friends, including me.
Come, lovers of ratatouille, and unite!

II

It is a sort of dream, which coincides
With the pacific relaxations called
Preferred Reality. Men who forget
Lovingly chopped-up cloves of *ail*, who scorn
The job of slicing two good peppers thinly,
Then two large onions and six aubergines –
Those long, impassioned and imperial purples –
Which, with six courgettes, you sift with salt
And cover with a plate for one round hour;
Or men who do not care to know about
The eight ripe *pommes d'amour* their wives have need of,
Preparing ratatouille, who give no thought to
The cup of olive oil that's heated in
Their heaviest pan, or onions, fried with garlic
For five observant minutes, before they add
Aubergines, courgettes, peppers, tomatoes;
Or men who give no thought to what their wives
Are thinking as they stand beside their stoves
When seasoning is sprinkled on, before
A *bouquet garni* is dropped in – these men
Invade Afghanistan, boycott the Games,
Call off their fixtures and prepare for war.

III

Cook for one hour, and then serve hot or cold.
Eat it, for preference, under the sun,
But, if you are Northern, you may eat
Your ratatouille imagining Provence.
Believe me, it goes well with everything,
As love does, as peace does, as summers do
Or any other season, as a lifetime does.

Acquire, then, for yourselves, ingredients;
Prepare this stew of love, and ask for more.
Quick, before it is too late. *Bon appetit*!

EUROPA'S LOVER

'Our Europe is not yours.'
Camus

'Men make more than one native land for themselves. There are some who feel at home in twenty corners of the world, for men are born more than once.'
Nizan

I

That beautiful lady walked
To the fragrant terrace
Of an especial hotel.
She walked out of the dusk
With Europe on her arm.

'Where are your shoes, Lady?
And your gown of silk,
This subtle décolletage,
Could not have been designed
In our provincial spa.'

'No,' she said. 'When my
Impeccable maternity
Concluded, my last child buried,
I had this made in Paris
By surrealist seamstresses.'

'Listen,' she said – you know
That listening tilt,
That smile on hearing far music? –
'These are the saxophones,
Far away, of the Riviera.'

'Sit by me,' said the Lady.
'You will suffer and travel
Thousands of years with me
Through my archives of sun and rain,
My annals of rivers and earth.'

II

'First, you must lose that obsession,'
She said, 'which deals in
Survival, prosperity and salvation.'

She showed me the waters of invitation,
Deep springs that coughed clear in the ground,
More solicitous than those
Thin, thermal pools, sipped at,
Bathed in and bottled in our matronly spa.

Debts were hushed in the bureaucracies.
Watery sunlight was a burst
Lit improvisation of liquid.
She scattered flowers on the water,
The mistress of her own rituals.

'Now you have died once, you will die again,
And live again. At your own funerals
You will stand among the trees
And grieve for your progency and future selves.'

III

Cold scholars in a christendom,
We are the children of children.
When was it in traditions that
We stopped living? When did we die?

Scriptoria furniture,
Oaken tables, oaken panels,
A trapped butterfly fluttering
Among the pedantry and heresies

In chained tomes, in motes of heart-dust . . .
An introspective summer illuminates
Tinted stories on the windows,
The gossip in the history of glass.
A narrative of colours spreads
On the blond stone, coagulated
Medieval light ruminating
Like abstract detectives on the slabs.
Lucid difficulties murmur
Contemplative stories of the West,
Martyrdoms, Reformations, Schisms.
Those finely carved mottoes
In delicate Latin are fading
As timber grows again
In a scriptorium bursting into leaf.
One more rub of an elbow,
Another scholar at this desk
Will return it to nature.
The inscriptions will float away
To Byzantine fastnesses
Or an islanded Irish hermitage.

IV

Many times we have risen
From the earthen delicatessen
Of the cemeteries, to tread
Moistened dust on city streets
Among litter, hand in hand,
Increasingly démodé, disappearing
Into salutations of light and water

At the foot of elaborate gardens
Where leaves are burned
In a dusk-rinsed smoke.

We are at home by nocturnal taxi ranks,
By the fast-food carts and chestnut hawkers
Ragged beside charcoal braziers
In these corners of metropolitan warmth.
We are at home among dandies
On the steps of the Opera House,
Among the crimson titles at passing-out parades
Or on the corners of unmapped rural lanes
Where wind meets us with a smell of cattle
And the scent of future rain.
We are at home in any occasion of
Citizens, urbanal and pastoral.

V

'What walks we have taken, together on
The verge of revealing our secrets,'
She said to me, incognito among
Market-stalls around a cathedral.

'We have seen the light-hearted
At their moderate courtships,
Whether pointing to the erotic stars
Or to the obese, detestable Zeppelins.

'In the fire-storms, love survived
And the terrorized hugged each other
To an inward collapse of hot char.
Silver birds of Imperial Airways flew

'From India with citizens and dossiers,
With brides flying to their weddings
High above the deserts, seas and ranges,
And even long armies and ferocious machines

'Failed to transform our favoured places,
And cruelty dies in the heart.
Still they come flying, and we welcome the dead
As they arrive to us in their wedding-clothes.'

VI

Shaped into this intimate suffering of death with life,
Past with present, living beneath a succession of coats
Until skin thickens into cloth, thread and blood, coarse
    immortality,
And blood thickens, and words melt on your tongue
As gourmet as a peppermint on a plate at Maxim's;
Shaped on a field behind the plough you were born to,
Shaped to these footprints, this size, in a drawing-room
Where you must sing before a brother of the bishop
Because aunt tells you to through her mouthful of cake;
Shaped as you sweep the gutter of its rejected trash –
How lonely is litter! – shaped as you sign a treaty
With the usurping nephew of a Maharajah or a Czar's
Bomb-crazy ambassador or a Kaiser's confidant;
Shaped before furnaces or dragging coal-carts with your
    back
In the mines of Yorkshire or Silesia, or shaped,
Shaped and indentured in the gardens of rhododendrons,
    peacocks
And exotic flora brought home by an eccentric uncle

Who commanded the firing-squads at Brazzaville or
    Hyderabad;
Shaped by decks and masts, spits and spars, that twiggery
Sprouting from warehouses before the continental wharfs;
Shaped by regiment; shaped by evictions, shaped by
Rhetorical prelates and their torturing sectaries;
Shaped in the moulds of foundries in Glasgow and
    Düsseldorf,
From cleared crofts in Sutherland to Fontamara, shaped,
Shaped, shaped and ruled, in kingdoms and palatinates, by
    archon,
By tyrant, by imperial whim gathering spiderwebs
To please Heliogabalus, by parliament, by Bourbon, by
    Tudor,
By Stuart, by Habsburg and Romanov, by democrat, by
    revolutionary
At his escritoire of apple-packings, by scythe and sabre,
By Capitalismus, by oligarch and plutocrat, by Socialismus,
By Trade, by Banks and by the algebra of money,
Shaped in battle or by a kiss, shaped in the bed of your
    parents,
Shaped to inherit or to labour in disciplined factories,
Shaped to administer in La Paz or Rangoon or the Islands...
All ways of being born, Europa, the chemistry of seed and
    cell,
And our millions plundered in their lands and cities,
Bullets searching them out like inquisitive half-wits from
The mitrailleuses of Europe, shreddings of men and women.
Now as two sit in a café in a French provincial town
Served by a descendant of métissage in Guadeloupe –
She is as beautiful as the wind on the Luberon –
There is no longer in our coffee that sensation of chains
    rattled

In offshore hulks, no longer in the sifts of our sugar
A slashing of docile machetes or orations by
Abolitionists in Chambers of Commerce. She is as beautiful
As those gone down in the chronicles of Jupiter,
    metamorphosis
And elegance, as beautiful as the classics of love and
    journeys,
As beautiful as any horseman from the eastern Steppes
Who nursed an arrow to a thong and raped the Empires.
Clocks, clocks, one era replaces another, and we are dressed
In history and shaped, shaped in days, peace and war,
In the circle of blood, in the races entwined like fingers.

VII

Time's information can be heard
In that withdrawal of sound,
Respiratory suck between each tock
In the numerical flower, the clock,
Christianity's chronometer.

Beyond tea-rooms and table manners,
Mendacities and instruments,
Above a mediocre autumn we
Revolve with fragments of
Immeasurable tragedy.

On the wristwatch of christendom,
In its little warehouse of Swiss seconds
Or in the lost shadows of sundials
Are the lives of millions, stored lives
With their unmeasured stories.

VIII

Relics of the Hanseatic
Where sea is sick of the oceanic
On toy ports of the Baltic Sea
A belch of herrings, a raft of timber

The waves beyond the links and marram
Tantalize a boy who would be an explorer
Leith, Danzig, Riga and Memel,
His nationality for ever, Bordeaux and Plymouth

Courage, sea folds on itself, sea on sea,
Layer upon layer in one wet seam
Each wave of the rose-less seas
Dark fjords dreaming of tropical yellow

The boy might stitch nets in Stornoway
Or die in the Grenadines, La Rochelle,
Cadiz and Genoa, or he might command
The wooden walls of Peter the Great

Or he might live in the stews of Tortuga, or
Deliver to the slave-jetties of San Domingo,
Composing hymns as the Africans
Enter the mysteries of economics

Demerara and Coromandel, Shanghai and San Francisco,
Icebergs, fogs, and the Newfoundland Banks,
Or he might sail to Celebes and Java,
Wading ashore to wave a cutlass at the pagodas

And the seas propose their liberty
On wandering routes that lead away from
Sugar, cotton, copra and geographies
Of skin and spice, silks, silver and gold

On further seas, where no fortune is found,
No maritime shortcut or adventure, but
The poetry of man in time and lonely space,
Where no fire has been lit, no language sung

Lisbon, Venice, Bristol, Glasgow and Marseilles,
Ghost-ships at the place without a name

IX

By the banks of a Scandinavian lake
We heard harness and smalltalk
As a migrating tribe came down
To water its ponies and say goodbye.

Later a picnic happened, with white cloths,
With children and jealousies and wine,
Women holding their skirts up to their knees
Tip-toeing over these same pebbles.

Then there was Strindberg or some such,
Up to his waist in lake and shivering,
Demented with ethics, maddened
By men and women and the snow falling.

X

It was the shape of her ankle
That first suggested I desired her.
So long ago now, I cannot remember
Her place, her time, or if she spoke to me.

There was a widow at an olive press
And a girl with a sketch pad I may have married,
A waitress singing alone among her tables,
A niece who combed her old aunt's tresses.

In my long visions I have seen them again
In their wedding-clothes, under the ground,
Their white dresses spread in the flowing earth,
In the warm, geological currents.

There was a boy who bathed my brow
Before the Sultan's janissaries came over
The rubbled citadel, and the girl I met
Beneath the chandeliers in Bucharest.

In love, I've felt love like anatomy
In meditation on itself, its real
And predatory contemplations, whether
Pure and languid or disturbed by lust.

Erotic, family Europe, full of your
Philosopher-uncles of the wedding-night,
We disperse to the genders, as fires
Burn down, like wine losing its red.

XI

I rang emaciated fens.
I rang the forests. I rang the sea.
With fingernail and numerals
I dialled the animals
And they were pleased to hear from me.

I sit beside the telephone
That speaks the truth, and speak to her
As winds converse with trees and grass.
Speak to me, Europa, of dear
Munificent existences.

Say nothing of the attainable to me.
I am tired of morals and commerce.
Say nothing of history.
Tell me of your new dress
And of the scandal of happiness.

XII

We heard the ghosts of Europe
On Danubian winds
Chattering of visits to
Shadowy Prague,
Krakow, Vienna, Paris,
Rome, and talking of
Carpathian wildflowers,
The gardeners of Picardy
And geriatric pro-consuls
On their bamboo chairs
In botanic country houses,

And of the magnates of
The Côte d'Ivoire and Java,
Resplendent among their trophies.

'I shall lead you,' she said,
'Along the path of graves
From Moscow to Calais
With many detours, touching
The shores of six seas.
Those huddled in pits,
In unmarked forest graves
Or in white fields
Of multiple crucifixion,
They are our people, too.
Released from nationality
They are fraternal
In the hoax of afterlife,
Snug among the alluvials
In the republic of Europe,
As, equal at last, they drain
Into Vistula and Rhine
And a thousand rivers,
The republic of wedding-clothes
Too many citizens to be
Cause of morbidity or grief,
Their lapsed literacies
Singing in earth and water
In all our languages.
Listen. They are reality.'

XIII

Exports of British, French,
Spaniards and Portuguese,
Exports of all Europe
For wealth and colonies,
From terror and pauperdom,
Dutch, German, Jew and Pole,
Sicilian and Florentine,
Magyar, Greek and Slav,
The Scandinavians.
Here is a photograph
Of a child burned by Americans.
They plundered his skin
For he was nowhere on
Their graph of dividends.
Of all the children in the world
He is the one with no mother.
Little victim, your eyes boiled;
You became a blister.
They are no different
From the barons of Europe –
Cossacks, dragoons, a sabre
For the relish of princes.
What are we now, who have friends,
Far kin breeding this America,
Bearing our names among
The enforced Africans
Named, too, for distant kin?
Little veteran, your pain
Has innocent predecessors
In maimed childhoods on
The streets and fields of here.

Laws, music and the Renaissance,
Sea-empires of the coolies,
Accomplishments and guilt
Propose a new devotion –
To tailoring and fountain-pens,
To the export of roses,
Artichokes, poetry,
A Western innocence.
Is it to have the spirit of sheep
To close our shops to
The sale of second-hand children?

XIV

We watched them go by, in the countryside,
The cities, in remote provincial districts,
The brides and grooms of wealth and poverty.
'The dead outnumber them, the living are
Such poor creatures. In time we shall retire
To my garden, to a beloved place
That is a museum of everywhere.
There are the equatorial sculptures from
Dahomey and Benin, and there are the dollars
Minted from Incan silver, there the cross
Worn by a priest martyred by Vandals,
A stone thrown at the time of the Fronde,
Skin flayed by the Inquisition and the eyes
Of Galileo. And if you listen you can hear
The dictionaries uttered on the air,
The music of Bach and Mozart, the rhymes of Dante
In my house built of night in the mountains
And in my house built of noon on the puszta.

I mean to be benevolent and wait.
We will till the sun and shade, for purity
And light are in themselves sufficient to us.
I shall re-write the books of equity,
Engender passion, justice, love and truth
And weave a fabric of persuasive virtue.
Sleep with me. You will be my many children,
My messenger and my amanuensis.
You have nothing to lose. Give me your life
Again, and again, as I invent my cause.
I am my own mother and my daughters.
I love my people. 'Our Europe is not yours.'
Together we will say that again, as, once,
It was said by one of my sons to another son
In the days of souls without names smouldering
In the years of the counting of rings and teeth.'

from ELEGIES

In memoriam
LESLEY BALFOUR DUNN
1944–1981

Salute, o genti umane affaticate!
Tutto trapassa e nulla può morir.
Noi troppo odiammo e sofferimmo. Amate.
Il mondo è bello e santo è l'avvenir.
                                        Carducci

Second Opinion

We went to Leeds for a second opinion.
After her name was called,
I waited among the apparently well
And those with bandaged eyes and dark spectacles.

A heavy mother shuffled with bad feet
And a stick, a pad over one eye,
Leaving her children warned in their seats.
The minutes went by like a winter.

They called me in. What moment worse
Than that young doctor trying to explain?
'It's large and growing.' 'What is?' 'Malignancy.'
'Why *there*? She's an artist!'

He shrugged and said, 'Nobody knows.'
He warned me it might spread. 'Spread?'
My body ached to suffer like her twin
And touch the cure with lips and healing sesames.

No image, no straw to support me – nothing
To hear or see. No leaves rustling in sunlight.
Only the mind sliding against events
And the antiseptic whiff of destiny.

Professional anxiety –
His hand on my shoulder
Showing me to the door, a scent of soap,
Medical fingers, and his wedding ring.

Thirteen Steps and the Thirteenth of March

She sat up on her pillows, receiving guests.
I brought them tea or sherry like a butler,
Up and down the thirteen steps from my pantry.
I was running out of vases.

More than one visitor came down, and said,
'Her room's so cheerful. She isn't afraid.'
Even the cyclamen and lilies were listening,
Their trusty tributes holding off the real.

Doorbells, shopping, laundry, post and callers,
And twenty-six steps up the stairs
From door to bed, two times thirteen's
Unlucky numeral in my high house.

And visitors, three, four, five times a day;
My wept exhaustions over plates and cups
Drained my self-pity in these days of grief
Before the grief. Flowers, and no vases left.

Tea, sherry, biscuits, cake, and whisky for the weak...
She fought death with an understated mischief –
'I suppose I'll have to make an effort' –
Turning down painkillers for lucidity.

Some sat downstairs with a hankie
Nursing a little cry before going up to her.
They came back with their fears of dying amended.
'Her room's so cheerful. She isn't afraid.'

Each day was duty round the clock.
Our kissing conversations kept me going,
Those times together with the phone switched off,
Remembering our lives by candlelight.

John and Stuart brought their pictures round,
A travelling exhibition. Dying,
She thumbed down some, nodded at others,
An artist and curator to the last,

Honesty at all costs. She drew up lists,
Bequests, gave things away. It tore my heart out.
Her friends assisted at this tidying
In a conspiracy of women.

At night, I lay beside her in the unique hours.
There were mysteries in candle-shadows,
Birds, aeroplanes, the rabbits of our fingers,
The lovely, erotic flame of the candlelight.

Sad? Yes. But it was beautiful also.
There was a stillness in the world. Time was out
Walking his dog by the low walls and privet.
There was anonymity in words and music.

She wanted me to wear her wedding ring.
It wouldn't fit even my little finger.
It jammed on the knuckle. I knew why.
Her fingers dwindled and her rings slipped off.

After the funeral, I had them to tea and sherry
At the Newland Park. They said it was thoughtful.
I thought it was ironic – one last time –
A mad reprisal for their loyalty.

Arrangements

'Is this the door?' This must be it. No, no.
We come across crowds and confetti, weddings
With well-wishers, relatives, whimsical bridesmaids.
Some have happened. Others are waiting their turn.
One is taking place before the Registrar.
A young groom is unsteady in his new shoes.
His bride is nervous on the edge of the future.
I walk through them with the father of my dead wife.
I redefine the meaning of 'strangers'.
Death, too, must have looked in on our wedding.
The building stinks of municipal function.
'Go through with it. You have to. It's the law.'
So I say to a clerk, 'I have come about a death.'
'In there,' she says. 'You came in by the wrong door.'

A woman with teenaged children sits at a table.
She hands to the clerk the paper her doctor gave her.
'Does that mean "heart attack"?' she asks.
How little she knows, this widow. Or any of us.
From one look she can tell I have not come
With my uncle, on the business of my aunt.
A flake of confetti falls from her fur shoulder.
There is a bond between us, a terrible bond
In the comfortless words, 'waste', 'untimely', 'tragic',
Already gossiped in the obit. conversations.
Good wishes grieve together in the space between us.
It is as if we shall be friends for ever
On the promenades of mourning and insurance,
In whatever sanatoria there are for the spirit,
Sharing the same birthday, the same predestinations.
Fictitious clinics stand by to welcome us,

Prefab'd and windswept on the edge of town
Or bijou in the antiseptic Alps,
In my case the distilled clinic of drink,
The clinic of 'sympathy' and dinners.

We enter a small office. 'What relation?' he asks.
So I tell him. Now come the details he asks for.
A tidy man, with small, hideaway handwriting,
He writes things down. He does not ask,
'Was she good?' Everyone receives this Certificate.
You do not need even to deserve it.
I want to ask why he doesn't look like a saint,
When, across his desk, through his tabulations,
His bureaucracy, his morbid particulars,
The local dead walk into genealogy.
He is no cipher of history, this one,
This recording angel in a green pullover
Administering names and dates and causes.
He has seen all the words that end in -oma.
'You give this to your undertaker.'

When we leave, this time it is by the right door,
A small door, taboo and second-rate.
It is raining. Anonymous brollies go by
In the ubiquitous urban drizzle.
Wedding parties roll up with white ribbons.
Small pools are gathering in the loving bouquets.
They must not see me. I bear a tell-tale scar.
They must not know what I am, or why I am here.
I feel myself digested in statistics of love.

Hundreds of times I must have passed this undertaker's
Sub-gothic premises with leaded windows,
By bus, on foot, by car, paying no attention.

We went past it on our first day in Hull.
Not once did I see someone leave or enter,
And here I am, closing the door behind me,
Turning the corner on a wet day in March.

France

A dozen sparrows scuttled on the frost.
We watched them play. We stood at the window,
And, if you saw us, then you saw a ghost
In duplicate. I tied her nightgown's bow.
She watched and recognized the passers-by.
Had they looked up, they'd know that she was ill –
'Please, do not draw the curtains when I die' –
From all the flowers on the windowsill.

'It's such a shame,' she said. 'Too ill, too quick.'
'I would have liked us to have gone away.'
We closed our eyes together, dreaming France,
Its meadows, rivers, woods and *jouissance*.
I counted summers, our love's arithmetic.
'Some other day, my love. Some other day.'

The Kaleidoscope

To climb these stairs again, bearing a tray,
Might be to find you pillowed with your books,
Your inventories listing gowns and frocks
As if preparing for a holiday.
Or, turning from the landing, I might find
My presence watched through your kaleidoscope,

A symmetry of husbands, each redesigned
In lovely forms of foresight, prayer and hope.
I climb these stairs a dozen times a day
And, by that open door, wait, looking in
At where you died. My hands become a tray
Offering me, my flesh, my soul, my skin.
Grief wrongs us so. I stand, and wait, and cry
For the absurd forgiveness, not knowing why.

Sandra's Mobile

A constant artist, dedicated to
Curves, shapes, the pleasant shades, the feel of colour,
She did not care what shapes, what red, what blue,
Scorning the dull to ridicule the duller
With a disinterested, loyal eye.
So Sandra brought her this and taped it up –
Three seagulls from a white and indoor sky –
A gift of old artistic comradeship.
'Blow on them, Love.' Those silent birds winged round
On thermals of my breath. On her last night,
Trying to stay awake, I saw love crowned
In tears and wooden birds and candlelight.
She did not wake again. To prove our love
Each gull, each gull, each gull, turned into dove.

Birch Room

Rotund and acrobatic tits explored
Bud-studded branches on our tallest birch tree,
A picture that came straight from her adored,
Delightfully composed chinoiserie.

She was four weeks dead before that first
Green haunting of the leaves to come, thickening
The senses with old hopes, an uncoerced
Surrender to the story of the Spring.

In summer, after dinner, we used to sit
Together in our second floor's green comfort,
Allowing nature and her modern inwit
Create a furnished dusk, a room like art.

'If only I could see our trees,' she'd say,
Bed-bound up on our third floor's wintry height.
'Change round our things, if you should choose to stay.'
I've left them as they were, in the leaf-light.

Tursac

Her pleasure whispered through a much-kissed smile.
'Oh, rock me firmly at a gentle pace!'
My love had lusty eagerness and style.
Propriety she had, preferring grace
Because she saw more virtue in its wit,
Convinced right conduct should have glamour in it
Or look good to an educated eye,
And never more than in those weeks of France
Perfected into rural elegance,

Those nights in my erotic memory.
I call that little house our *Thébaïde*
(The literary French!), and see her smile,
Then hear her in her best sardonic style:
'Write out of me, not out of what you read.'

Empty Wardrobes

I sat in a dress shop, trying to look
As dapper as a young ambassador
Or someone who'd impressed me in a book,
A literary rake or movie star.

Clothes are a way of exercising love.
False? A little. And did she like it? Yes.
Days, days, romantic as Rachmaninov,
A ploy of style, and now not comfortless.

She walked out from the changing-room in brown,
A pretty smock with its embroidered fruit;
Dress after dress, a lady-like red gown
In which she flounced, a smart career-girl's suit.

The dress she chose was green. She found it in
Our clothes-filled cabin trunk. The pot-pourri,
In muslin bags, was full of where and when.
I turn that scent like a memorial key.

But there's that day in Paris, that I regret,
When I said No, franc-less and husbandly.
She browsed through hangers in the Lafayette,
And that comes back tonight, to trouble me.

Now there is grief the couturier, and grief
The needlewoman mourning with her hands,
And grief the scattered finery of life,
The clothes she gave as keepsakes to her friends.

Creatures

A lime tree buzzed with its remembered bees.
We stood on the terrace. Fanatic prayers
Rattled with resigned displeasure. Martyrs!
'Ave!' Grasshoppers. Insect rosaries.

Nervously proud, itself, and secular,
A fox patrolled on its instinctive route
Past us and nut trees to the absolute
Wild pathless woods, a French fox, pure *renard*.

Hérisson and the encyclopaedic owl
Plotted the earth and sky of dusk. Oldest
Inhabited valley – we felt it blessed
By creatures and impacted human soul.

She said, 'The world is coming out tonight.'
Vézère's *falaises* moved grey; an ivied mist
Disguised the distance and we stood, our trust
In lizards, settling birds, the impolite

Belettes, the heavy hornets and the truths
Compiling in our senses, plain, of this life,
If inarticulate. I loved my wife.
Our two lives fluttered like two windowed moths.

She was the gentlest creature of them all.
She scattered milk-dipped bread for the lazy snakes
Asleep in the Mouliniers' bramble-brakes.
I asked her, 'Why?' 'It's only natural.'

A paradisal stasis filled the dark.
She scattered bread. 'A snake's a shy creature.'
I dip my bread in milk, and I think of her,
The châtelaine of her reasonable ark.

At the Edge of a Birchwood

Beneath my feet, bones of a little bird
Snap in a twig-flutter. A hundred wings
Adore its memory, and it is heard
In the archival choirs now where it sings.

Ewes nurse their lamb-flock on an upland field.
Late gambols in the last kick of the sun
As I scoop dirt on a hand's weight, briefly held,
A cradled cup of feathered, egg-shelled bone,

Turning the earth on it; and underground
Go song and what I feel, go common things
Into the cairn of a shoe-patted mound,
Goes half my life, go eyes, instinct and wings.

The moon rubs through the blue pallor of high east
And childlessness has no number in the May
Shadowed with birchlight on the county's crest.
This year her death-date fell on Mother's Day.

The Clear Day

Sunlight gathers in the leaves, dripping
Invisible syrups. Long afternoons
Have been reduced to this significant
Table, melodious ice cubes shaken in
A blue tumbler, lazily tipped vermouth
And a hand measuring it, a propped elbow,
A languid eye, while a reflection on
A leaf turns into everything called summer.
The heat haze ripples through the far away
Gardens of strangers, acquaintances, of those
I can put a face to. With my eyes shut,
Squeezing the soft salts of their sweat, I see
Beyond my body, nerves, cells, brain, and leisure.
Blue coastal persons walk out of the haze.
They have outflown the wind, outswum the sea.
I think, and feel, and do, but do not know
All that I am, all that I have been, once,
Or what I could be could I think of it.
These blue pedestrians bruised the edge of me
To a benign remorse, with my lessons.
With my eyes shut, I walk through a wet maze
Following a thread of sounds – birdsong in
Several cadences, children, a dog-bark,
The traffic roaring against silence as
A struck match drowns it out, simple tunes of
An amateur pianist, a vulgar shout,
A bottle tapped against a thirsty glass,
The burst of its pouring, and the slip
When the chilled glass wets a wet lower lip.
I could not guess at what the pictures are
In the eyes of a friend turned round to watch

Shrub shadows dapple a few yards of lawn
As his smoke clings to his thoughtful posture.
Tonight, I shall look out at the dark trees,
Writing this in the muddle of lost tenses
At an o'clock of flowers turned colourless.
Then, as always, the soul plays over mind
With radiantly painful speculations.
I shall sieve through our twenty years, until
I almost reach the sob in the intellect,
The truth that waits for me with its loud grief,
Sensible, commonplace, beyond understanding.

A Summer Night

Dusk softens round the leaf and cools the West.
Rhythmical fragrances, wind, grass and leaves,
Fly in and out on scented cadences.
I go into the bedroom of the world,
Discovering the long night of my life.
This telephone is electronic lies,
Ringing with calls, with farewells of the dead
Paid for on credit. Nocturnal postmen ring
My doorbell; I refuse to let them in.
My birch trees have their own two lives to lead
Without our love, although we named them us.
They play inside the aromatic wind
That is their house for ever. Outside time,
On the sensation of a memory
I walk through the dark house, remembering.
I meet the seasons on the stairs, breathing
Their pulchritudes, their four degrees of heat,
Four shades of day, shade on shade, shade on shade.

I have gone through a year, in at one end,
Out at the same way in. Same every year,
But that year was different. I counted days
As Francis counted sparrows, being kind to them.
They were not kind to me. My floating life
Borrows its fortitude from a cool silence
Composed of green, from two trees, from the tingle
That was the touch of us against the world.
It left its lived heat everywhere we'd been,
A small white cry, one last wild, stubborn rose.

Reincarnations

The kitten that befriends me at its gate
Purrs, rubs against me, until I say goodbye,
Stroking its coat, and asking 'Why? Why? Why?'
For now I know the shame of being late
Too late. She waits for me at home
Tonight, in the house-shadows. And I must mourn
Until Equator crawls to Capricorn
Or murder in the sun melts down
The Arctic and Antarctica. When bees collide
Against my study's windowpane, I let them in.
She nurtures dignity and pride;
She waters in my eye. She rustles in my study's palm;
She is the flower on the geranium.
Our little wooden train runs by itself
Along the windowsill, each puff-puff-puff
A breath of secret, sacred stuff.
I feel her goodness breathe, my Lady Christ.
Her treasured stories mourn her on their shelf,
In spirit-air, that watchful poltergeist.

Reading Pascal in the Lowlands

His aunt has gone astray in her concern
And the boy's mum leans across his wheelchair
To talk to him. She points to the river.
An aged angler and a boy they know
Cast lazily into the rippled sun.
They go there, into the dappled grass, shadows
Bickering and falling from the shaken leaves.

His father keeps apart from them, walking
On the beautiful grass that is bright green
In the sunlight of July at 7 p.m.
He sits on the bench beside me, saying
It is a lovely evening, and I rise
From my sorrows, agreeing with him.
His large hand picks tobacco from a tin;

His smile falls at my feet, on the baked earth
Shoes have shuffled over and ungrassed.
It is discourteous to ask about
Accidents, or of the sick, the unfortunate.
I do not need to, for he says 'Leukaemia'.
We look at the river, his son holding a rod,
The line going downstream in a cloud of flies.

I close my book, the *Pensées* of Pascal.
I am light with meditation, religiose
And mystic with a day of solitude.
I do not tell him of my own sorrows.
He is bored with misery and premonition.
He has seen the limits of time, asking 'Why?'
Nature is silent on that question.

A swing squeaks in the distance. Runners jog
Round the perimeter. He is indiscreet.
His son is eight years old, with months to live.
His right hand trembles on his cigarette.
He sees my book, and then he looks at me,
Knowing me for a stranger. I have said
I am sorry. What more is there to say?

He is called over to the riverbank.
I go away, leaving the Park, walking through
The Golf Course, and then a wood, climbing,
And then bracken and gorse, sheep pasturage.
From a panoptic hill I look down on
A little town, its estuary, its bridge,
Its houses, churches, its undramatic streets.

Land Love

We stood here in the coupledom of us.
I showed her this – a pool with leaping trout,
Split-second saints drawn in a rippled nimbus.

We heard the night-boys in the fir trees shout.
Dusk was an insect-hovered dark water,
The calling of lost children, stars coming out.

With all the feelings of a widower
Who does not live there now, I dream my place.
I go by the soft paths, alone with her.

Dusk is a listening, a whispered grace
Voiced on a bank, a time that is all ears
For the snapped twig, the strange wind on your face.

She waits at the door of the hemisphere
In her harvest dress, in the remote
Local August that is everywhere and here.

What rustles in the leaves, if it is not
What I asked for, an opening of doors
To a half-heard religious anecdote?

Monogamous swans on the darkened mirrors
Picture the private grace of man and wife
In its white poise, its sleepy portraitures.

Night is its Dog Star, its eyelet of grief
A high, lit echo of the starry sheaves.
A puff of hedge-dust loosens in the leaves.
Such love that lingers on the fields of life!

Home Again

Autumnal aromatics, forgotten fruits
In the bowl of this late November night,
Chastise me as I put my suitcase down.
The bowl's crystal shines and feels like frost,
And these have been the worst days of its life.
Cadaver orchard, an orphanage of pips,
Four apples sink into a pulpy rust,
And *Eat me, eat me*, says a withered pear,
Pay for your negligence and disrespect.
A scent of Burgundy – a bunch of grapes
Drinking their mortuary juice, their wrinkled skins
Dwindled and elderly black emaciations.
My six weeks gone from home portray the days
On stopped clocks and a vegetable absence.

Throw out the green loaf and bacterial cheese,
Shrunk carrots and potatoes begging for earth.
It is very lonely on the green settee,
Under the lamp, with my breath visible.
The curtains dangle in a window-sway,
In window-cold. I touch their foliage,
Their textile, sympathetic park.
I have been there in dreams, walking among
Peach-groves, and dressed in raiment of the East
In vineyards overlaid with Martagon lilies,
Arabic gardens, the south of Summerland.
Warmth is beginning and the pipes shudder.
I taste my house. Each day of its hungry gnosis,
It led a life of its own, empty of me.
The moon's oasis, the moon sipped the fruit
And the dust settled and thickened, the cold
Entered books and furniture, china and cushions.
My open suitcase mocks me from the floor.
The room is an aghast mouth. Its kiss is cold.
I think of a piano with its lid locked
And a carved, ivory silence in it.
I look at a vase. It is too much to bear,
For it speaks of a deranged expiry,
An accusation of browned leafage.
I see the falling off of its petals
In a flashback of flowers, the white zig-zags,
A snowfall of botanic ecstasy.
A spirit shivers in the appled air,
And I know whose it is. A floral light
Bleaches my eyes with angelophanous
Secrets. They are more than remembering,
Larger than sentiment. I call her name,
And it is very strange and wonderful.

The Stories

No longer are there far-flung outposts of Empire
    Where a heartsore widower could command a wall
Against the hairy raiders ignorant of commerce.
    Too much morality has interposed
Its wishy-washy journalism and hope. Who am I
    To weep for Salvador or Kampuchea
When I am made the acolyte of my own shadow?
    Grief has its own romance, its comedy,
Its preposterous and selfish gestures. Men and women,
    Who, one day, will feel as I do now, I
Empty my heart, my head, dreaming again of days
    Gone by in another life. I could sail North
To Spitzbergen, to the iced-over mountainous islands
    Outlined on charts of the glacial deltas,
Or south to the rainforests, or to the blank of sands
    Drifting like the heartlessness of time.
Where is the frontier I could serve with a paid sword
    Dutiful to an imperial ass who lavishes
His days on orthodox, abstruse theology
    And his exchequer on a paradise
To please the gluttony of his heretical consort?
    At my age, I could die splendidly on
A staircase, unarmed, banished, but soldierly, before
    The spears and sabres of the wicked host
That trumped my preparations and stole the city
    In the name of their Prophet. I could have died
On the trails of exploration, under the sun or the arrows.
    And what religion is left now, to serve
With local Caledonian sainthood, stern, but kind,
    Baptizing the baby Africans, and plodding
To a discovery of God and waterfalls?

Nor are there any longer those unvisited isles
Where a beachcomber might scrounge a boozy salvation.
    To meditate in a tropical hovel –
Palm leaves, creeper, cocunt shells, jettisoned containers –
    On wheretofores, buts, ifs and perhapses,
Over that anguished prose of what we think we deserve,
    Or don't deserve, but live with, either way,
Would be a perfect if anti-social philosophizing,
    Doubtless illogical, or arrogant,
Or windily puffed-up to heights of self-deception.
    Interior ethics, like oncogenic catastrophes,
Happen anywhere, the melanomas of the sun
    Or the occult surprises of contemplation.
Why grieve like this? I loathe my bitter, scorning wit,
    This raffish sorrow artificed by stories.
I can see myself in a jungle-drunk's smeared linen suit
    Under the fan in a lost trading post,
Most Maugham-ish in my matutinal repartee
    At my breakfast of mango and whisky
As the steamer arrives, delicate with white nuns
    And crates of Haig and quinine, the new clerk
Already mothered on the rack of a malarial fever.
    There are a thousand plots in the narrative
In which grief is the hero. In these frequent stories
    There is always somewhere to go to, outbacks,
Exiles, White Men's Graves where piratical gun-runners
    Mix with evangelists, where wilderness
Brings out the worst of men as well as charity,
    Where sacrifice embroiders every tale
And the devoted nun weeps in the shot-up pagoda
    As a Chicagoan's lung-blood soaks her arms.
Breast-plated with Gustavus Adolphus and Dalgetty,
    I could have lost myself in Baltic syntax.

Foot-slogging the Sahara with kepi, pack and gun,
    I could have made the beautiful gesture,
The joke of spitting in Death's broad, fictitious grin.
    It is no longer the world of the stories.
Opportunities for a ludicrous public service,
    For the lunacy of last-ditch duty
To Monarch, regiment or John Company,
    Are stoic options stored in Yesterday.
Why be discreet? A broken heart is what I have –
    A pin to burst the bubble of shy poetry,
Mnemosyne revealed as what, in life, she stands for.
    I shall observe the moods of the great sky,
The flight of herons, the coming into leaf of birches
    And the religious glow on ancient waves
Breaking against *Candida casa* of the cliffs.
    If you should see me, or one of my kind,
Looking out to the far ocean from a lonely headland,
    Or walking by the hedgerows, then turn away.
Walk on by, and leave us there to remember and dream
    Our speculative visions of the past
Narrated through the legendary, retrospective fictions,
    Tales of anachronism. Such days they were!
Not even that sweet light garnishing Sisyphean innocence
    Redeems me, dedicated to the one
Pure elegy, looking as if I like the way I am.
    I do not; for I would rather that I could die
In the act of giving, and prove the truth of us
    Particular, eternal, by doing so
Be moral at the moment of the good death, showing
    An intimate salvation beyond the wish
Merely to die, but to be, for once, commendable.

Anniversaries

Day by nomadic day
Our anniversaries go by,
Dates anchored in an inner sky,
To utmost ground, interior clay.
   It was September blue
When I walked with you first, my love,
In Roukenglen and Kelvingrove,
Inchinnan's beech-wood avenue.
   That day will still exist
Long after I have joined you where
Rings radiate the dusty air
And bangles bind each powdered wrist.
   Here comes that day again.
What shall I do? Instruct me, dear,
Longanimous encourager,
Sweet Soul in the athletic rain
   And wife now to the weather.

   Glaswegian starlings fly
In their black cape, a fluttered noise,
Ornithological hurrahs
From spires in the November sky.
   The Candleriggs is husks
And cabbage leaves, a citric scent,
A vegetable sentiment,
Closed apple-depots in the dusk's
   Indigenous metaphor –
Arcadian orchards of the lost
On this Bohemian sea-coast
And exits, pursued by a bear.
   I passed our wedding day

Drunk on the salad street, a null
White-out of loss and alcohol;
Your ring, our anniversary,
    And starlings in my soul.

    A liquid light sips dew
From how it is as blossoms foam
With May's arboreal aplomb
Against a reminiscent blue.
    Day, number, memory,
Kissed hours when day's door hangs ajar
And light crawls on the calendar,
Each routine anniversary
    At night, and noon, and dawn,
Are times I meet you, when souls rinse
Together in their moist reunions.
Iambic, feathery Anon
    Opens anthologies,
Born and reborn, as days go by
In anniversaries of sky
When oceans cradle little seas
    That water in the eye.

    My diaries are days,
Flesh days and real. The calendar
Recurs to tell us who we are,
Or were, to praise or to dispraise.
    Here is a day come round
Again. This window's a wet stone
I can't see through. Daylight and sun,
Reflectionless, a glassy ground,
    It slides on vitreous space.
I shiver in the memory
And sculpt my foolish poetry

From thwarted life and snapped increase.
  Cancer's no metaphor.
Bright rain-glass on the window's birch
This supernatural day of March,
  Dwindled, come dusk, to one bright star,
  Cold and compassionate.

Hush

Shh. Sizzle of days, weeks, months, years...
How much of us has gone, rising and crying.
My skin seeps its pond of dew.

Air sips and licks as I walk out today
In the transparent jaw of the weather
When the first leaves are greening.

Behind me I can hear
A click of fantasy heels,
But there is no one there.

She is with me, as I call to see
A sick friend whose skin is drying
On the bones of her spirit.

I stand on the sad threshold with my flowers.
How old this is, and how the heart beats faster
As I wait at the bell like a mourning wooer,

As the dog barks, as I give my flowers
And a secret wind blows in from eternal woods,
As my flowers sigh, asking for water.

Leaving Dundee

A small blue window opens in the sky
As thunder rumbles somewhere over Fife.
Eight months of up-and-down – goodbye, goodbye –
Since I sat listening to the wild geese cry
Fanatic flightpaths up autumnal Tay,
Instinctive, mad for home – make way! make way!
Communal feathered scissors, cutting through
The grievous artifice that was my life,
I was alert again, and listening to
That wavering, invisible V-dart
Between two bridges. Now, in a moistened puff,
Flags hang on the château-stacked gables of
A 1980s expense account hotel,
A lost French fantasy, baronial.
From here, through trees, its Frenchness hurts my heart.
It slips into a library of times.
Like an eye on a watch, it looks at me.
And I am going home on Saturday
To my house, to sit at my desk of rhymes
Among familiar things of love, that love me.
Down there, over the green and the railway yards,
Across the broad, rain-misted, subtle Tay,
The road home trickles to a house, a door.
She spoke of what I might do 'afterwards'.
'Go, somewhere else.' I went north to Dundee.
Tomorrow I won't live here any more,
Nor leave alone. *My love, say you'll come with me.*

from NORTHLIGHT

At Falkland Palace

For L.J.B.

Innermost dialect
Describes Fife's lyric hills,
Life, love and intellect
In lucid syllables,
  Domestic air.
Natural play of sun and wind
Collaborates with leaf and mind,
  The world a sentient
  Botanic instrument,
    Visible prayer.
  Everything's birth begins
  On the moment of the May's
  Creaturely origins
  – I'll live for these good days
    Love leads me to
In gardened places such as this
Of the flower and apple-promise,
  Lark-sung, finch-wonderful;
  Edenic circumstance, not fall,
    Walking with you.
  Balladic moments pass,
  Tongue-tied, parochial,
  A narrative of grass
  And stone's hierarchical
    Scottish Versailles.

These native liberties propose
Our lives, rose by unbudding rose,
    A song-crazed laverock
    Whose melodies unlock
        Audible sky.

    Dynastic stonework flakes,
    Weathers and fails, withdraws
    From shapely time and shakes
    A gargoyle's severed claws
        At visitors.
Here wrinkled time's abolished house
Perpetuates a posthumous
    Nation, monarchy's urn
    In which the Stewarts mourn
        What once was theirs.
    In a country like this
    Our ghosts outnumber us:
    A ruined artifice
    Empty and sonorous,
        Malevolent
In how its past force-feeds with filth
Anachronism's commonwealth
    And history bemoans
    What history postpones,
        The true event.
    In the hollows of home
    I find life, love and ground
    And intimate welcome:
    With you, and these, I'm bound
        To history.

Touching your hair, holding your hand,
Your beauty blends with time and land,
    And you are loveliness
    In your green, country dress,
        So fair this day.

Love-making by Candlelight

Skin looked like this two hundred years ago
When candlelight lapped the erotic straw
In hilly farms where windowed candlefire
Burnished imperfect glass. Portending haws
Hung on the leafless bush, amazement's bud
Red on the acres of nocturnal snow
As uplands rose to tufted winterlight,
In their celestial altitude
The eighteenth-century stars.

This is how it must be, shape-shifting fire's
Impatient nudity and ours
On the big bed. A molten vividness
Dismantles gender and the way it moves
Identifies a married venery
Timeless in the bedroom of the species –
A Pictish smile, a medieval kiss,
A whispered pre-industrial draught
On our contemporary bed.

Played on by fire, those clustered cornice grapes
Outwit their plaster: cornucopia's vine,
Pompeian opulence, rumours
From far back, echoes of Florentine
Intrigue, Renaissance footsteps in the hall

Where gossips overhear indelible
Echoed courtships; and these Muscovian furs
Were linen until fire reshaped
Their transient destiny.

Hands dipped in light-and-shadow cast
Ledas and satyrs on the bedroom wall.
A candleflame's a silent chatterbox
And cinematic book: bestiary candle,
History candle, yellow metaphor,
Venereal fire. Open the curtains now
And add a star to what we do and say
Past midnight in our only country,
Our private anywhere.

Who else is looking at the Firth tonight
Drowsy with afterlove? Local Tristan,
Indigenous Iseult, and Dido sees
Aeneas in a navigation light.
Dog-collared Abelard walks Heloise
Among the gravestones, yews and cypresses.
An Orphic nightbird cries 'Eurydice'...
Love, touch my heart with who you are
And sleep, history, sleep.

S. Frediano's

S. Frediano is St Finnian
Who spelled the rivers with his wand of faith,
The Ayrshire Garnoch and the streams of Down.

He brought his water-miracles to Tuscany,
Turning the Serchio with a little rake,
Praying, perhaps, when it was done, in Gaelic.

Lucca was lonely but not foreign
Far from his college on the coast of Solway,
Candida casa's Gallovidian stone.

He lies under the high altar
In a faint aroma of cypress,
His bones united by fine silver wires.

It is cool and dark in S. Frediano's church.
Parishioners pray in its visited sanctity,
Listless, pious, old, *simpatico*.

Tourists listen in on telephones
To stories in the language of their choice.
There is that smell of medieval history.

I hear a bird high in a vitreous blur
Singing its song of the sacred windows,
Its coincidental literature.

S. Zita, mummified, is dressed
For blessed waltzing when the trumpets sound.
Her skin is fastened like a frozen dust,

Her fingerjoints a grey bamboo,
Her gown a lace spun by celestial spiders,
Bridal, bizarre, miraculous.

In her glass coffin, she exhibits
Centuries of death that mount and mount.
Light Italian lire clink in the coinboxes.

It is a human place – a tourist
Stooped in a pose of scholarly inspection;
A couple who light candles for their dead

And who have yet to read
S. Frediano learned his miracles
In places they came here to be away from.

The People Before

I've turned my back on Tuesday's half-past four
As 1985's obscured momentum
Falters towards the closing of an epoch.
Crepuscular, two tradesmen, walking home,
Know that they're woodcuts by a local master,
Firm local lines, modernity unstuck.

Migrating geese, in an up-ended V,
Caricature my watch's measurement,
Half-past the hour and continuity
In sepia, any time but this
Post-dated country etched in aquatint
Nearing the day of luck and all good wishes.

Streetlamps come on.
Frock-coated decades trespass on the tense.
Spent eras stain
Anachronistic stone –
Luminous echoes, gaslit reminiscence,
Distorted, thinned, Victorian.

A push can coax our gate
Into releasing an Edwardian squeak.
December's frozen rose
Nods to unseen applause.
A sparrow lifts its startled featherweight
And petals tumble in a cruel slapstick.

Preliminary moonlight on the Firth
Casts in-betweenness on the time and light –
Not now, not then, not day, not night,
But moonlight's childhood, waterworn;
And, in one moment, all death, all birth,
All dying and being reborn.

Beyond our neighbours' frosted washing-lines,
Their silvered slates and chimneypots,
Our borderland begins
As light withdraws to loss of Monifieth,
Subplots and counterplots
Narrated in the coastline's myth.

Make what you can of it, for no one knows
What story's told by winter-misted hills
Or how a river flows
Against the tide in white scribbles.
A patiently daemonic frost
Sharpens its needles on the eastern coast.

Processionals of lives go by
On delicate, crisp treads;
Blurred fragrances, gently percussive,
Stir among leaves.
Top-hatted heads of firms and kitchen-maids
Visit the instincts of the eye.

Swish, hush and microsound, the whispered *ahs*,
Converse with silence's midpoint
Over the Firth, and time is disobedient,
Mixing its years and generations.
It's 1940 on the weatherglass
And now and then in the events of nations.

Night swells with navigation's stars
Honed to a masterpiece of quiet.
Dismantled commerce hungers for its jute,
Esparto, timber, coal and mariners,
Prosperity and credit.
Lighthouses warn the swimmers on a lost trade route.

A candleflame, held by a child
Walking past, reddens a window, her face
A spectral captive in the window's glass,
Her neck a ruff of fiery nightgown lace.
Coniferous estates, the winterfield,
Submerge their farms in foliage and grass.

More geese rant westward, flock by chevroned flock.
The house of us now, love, of you and me.
I turn a blacksmithed key in its lock.
Feeling its freezing metal on their hands,
These other people turned this iron key.
The lunar honey fell on Buddon Sands.

February

Maternal in the glow of shaded light,
Your smile has proved the truth of love tonight,
Holding the hunger of our much-loved child
Who lately in his father's arms was held.

Daylight

The big white arms of dawn are cool
In their embrace, and merciful
First blue dispels the estuary's
Possessive, tenemented greys.
The gleam on Buddon Ness protects
Survival where sunlight reacts
With sand and private history,
With window-coloured dawn and sea.
Enormous world, this little place
Observes its vulnerable trace
On time, topography and globe,
Its rooftops polished in the scrub
Of climbing sunlight, while the gleam
On Buddon Ness persists, a dream
In sleepy eyes at windows where
Early risers pause and stare
At distances beyond their town,
And someone in a dressing-gown
Eavesdrops as mysteries discuss
Sung mornings to no human purpose.
Wordless symposia, in tongues
Informed beyond mere rights and wrongs;
Luminous discourse, shade by shade,

Its meanings light-and-water-made
Or turned by wind and by what happens
Into a foliated sense –
A mind could catch at them, and try
To understand that dot of sky
Balanced on Buddon's easternmost
Outreach of military coast
Transmitting random ironies
Out of the library of days.
I've seen a star poised on the tip
Of a still leaf, pure partnership
Here makes with there and everywhere
Between life, death and forever.
Last night in Tayport, leaf and star
– Still, very still – melted together
In life's delight and woke to this
Lucidity and genesis,
A wordlight in the watery grey,
Sinister, thrawn, the estuary
A colourless mirroring stone,
Offensive, querulous, sullen;
And then daylight on Buddon Ness,
Curative, clear and meaningless.

Going to Aberlemno

By archaeologies of air,
Folkways of kirks and parishes
Revised by salty haar,
You reach the previous
Country, the picturesque
And the essential east,

By a padlocked summer kiosk
And industry's ill-starred
Inlets, a breaker's-yard
A ruby sore of rust.
Here four roads intersect
Beside the tallest oak
And the best hawthorn
Where every step you take
Breaks on an acorn.
Through astral solitude
A Pictish dialect,
Above a bridged Firth, cries
For lyric nationhood,
And horsemen, in a stone disguise,
Ride through the Pictish wood.

Abernethy

Air-psalters and pages of stone
Inscribed and Caledonian
Under these leaf-libraries where
Melodious lost literature
Remembers itself! A white
Dove climbs on its Columban flight
In the botanic radiance,
Northlight's late druidic rinse
Lapping against time and earth
In this root view of Fife and Perth.
A thousand years of briars enclose
A wild and matrilinear rose
Whose house began before the oak
First felt the axeman's stroke.

An unrecorded Kentigern
Disturbs a prehistoric fern
And hours from the Pictavian clock
Measure the lives of land and rock
And miles before the pedlared road
Winds to Iona and to God.

Out of the thanages, mormaerdoms,
Legendary shires and kingdoms,
Defunct boundaries and the lost
Dynastic certainties – a ghost
Light on the grass, a shivering
Transparent wing.
Listen to twigs scratch as a broom
Swishes across a vanished room
Trembling on this venerable
And enigmatic hill.
At the time when our names began
In the years of the Dark Age swan
And the wolf, on hills like this one,
A herdsman looked over and down
On blue waters in the strath.
This moment is his aftermath
Also, a lived and living scent
Scattering and ever-present,
As are the lady and her hind
Fragments of spirit, leaf and mind.

75°

Delayed by southern possessiveness,
The summer's agents turn up late
With their sorries, their more-or-less
Sincere apologies, lightweight
Attire, ubiquitous assistants
Performing aerial events,
Weavers of avian cradles where
A byre or gable tucks the air
Under its eaves. 'What kept you, friends?'
Bavarian asparagus,
Burgundian grapes and other godsends,
The usual Hispanic fuss,
Devonian nativities
Beginning in the apple trees.
The glass farms of the Netherlands
Commanded sun and tied our hands.
'At least, you've come. Our bad selves, dulled
By winter and frustrated spring,
Drained good from us, and poured a cold
Malevolence over everything.'

II

We tend our earthen restaurants,
Buying our portions of the south;
Strange languages visit our tongues,
Saying 'I love you', mouth to mouth.
Erotic gardens promise fruit
Nurtured from an ancestral root.
A smile, and the clematis flowers.

[175]

A few weeks more, and south is ours!
Yachts multiply; pods flex
Deserved and succulent harvests.
Lawn-mowers, shirt-sleeves, open necks...
Young girls ring daisies round their wrists.
Mrs Belle Gilsand's parrot squawks
For liberty beyond her clock's
North-facing mantelpiece – humdrum,
Tick-tocking tropic martyrdom.
Deep in coniferous woods, the dry
Needle blankets shift, claw and squall
Shaded by wing-beats, then a shy
Creaturely panic and paw-fall.

III

Eat fern seed, walk invisible.
Summer is fragrant this far north.
By night, on Inverdovat's hill,
Visit the gods of wood and Firth
By paths of inner wanderlust
Here on the summer's Pictish Coast
Where half-forgotten festivals
Quicken the half-remembering pulse.
Watch starlight struggle in an oak's
Irradiated rafters, hear
A minstrelsy from lunar hammocks
Sing love songs to the hemisphere.
Moonbathe, be moonstruck, watch a birch
Assume serenity and search
For its perfection, northern
On its grass sofa, turf and moon-fern
Delighted where a foot-snapped twig

Startles symphonic foliage
And mushrooms tremble on their log,
Stellar on an eternal ridge.

IV

The heart stays out all night. Each house
A variant of moonlit slates
And flightpaths of the flittermouse,
Sleeps in the dream it illustrates
Translating garden laureates
Into unlettered alphabets,
Holding antiquity and now
Within the same nocturnal vow –
Internal wonders in that pale
Hour after sunset when you hear
A visionary nightingale
Articulate your life's frontier.
An owl perched on a chimneypot
Too-woos its legendary thought
Across the estuary of dream
Along the light-buoy's punctual beam.
Stars in the trees, moon on a headstone,
Night's footprints on the riddled earth;
The wind's herbaceous undertone,
Moon-puddled water, mystic Firth ...

V

Planthouses force Italian heat
On melon, pepper, peach and vine
And horticultural conceit
Perfects a Scottish aubergine.
Imagination manufactures

A vitreous continent, nature's
Geography turned inside out
On the botanic roundabout.
By fraudulent, glass-roofed lagoons
Gardeners ply the trowel and hoe
On Polynesian afternoons
Of the oriole and the papingo.
Waterfalls slacken, their cold threads
Dribble on shrunken riverbeds.
There's trouble at the reservoir:
At night it launders one pale star.
Dry pelts diminish on the road,
Each beast its dehydrated shroud;
A butterfly's life-episode
Withers in daylong adulthood.

VI

Postponed by seasonal delight
And midnight sun, the north returns,
A furred, Icelandic anchorite
Travelling south by landmarked cairns,
Islands, headlands, bearing his cold
Autumnal charms, spelling ridged gold
Into the shiver in the leaf,
Deciduous, wrinkled and skew-whiff.
Rumoured by clouds and sudden chills,
By falls of apple, plum and pear,
Arched, orphaned cats on window-sills
And by botanic disrepair –
Look to your blessings and your coat,
Gloves for your hands, a scarf for your throat.
Your gardens, yielding pod by pod,

Surrender to another god.
Go home; chop wood. North-easters strain
Over the sea. Farewell. This line –
Greybreaking, late September rain –
Falls heavy, cold, and argentine.

Tay Bridge

A sky that tastes of rain that's still to fall
And then of rain that falls and tastes of sky ...
The colour of the country's moist and subtle
In dusk's expected rumour. Amplify
All you can see this evening and the broad
Water enlarges, Dundee slips by an age
Into its land before the lights come on.
Pale, mystic lamps lean on the river-road
Bleaching the city's lunar after-image,
And there's the moon, and there's the setting sun.

The rail bridge melts in a dramatic haze.
Slow visibility – a long train floats
Through a stopped shower's narrow waterways
Above rose-coloured river, dappled motes
In the eye and the narrow piers half-real
Until a cloud somewhere far in the west
Mixes its inks and draws iron and stone
In epic outlines, black and literal.
Now it is simple, weathered, plain, immodest
In waterlight and late hill-hidden sun.

High water adds freshwater-filtered salt
To the aquatic mirrors, a thin spice
That sharpens light on Middle Bank, a lilt

In the reflected moon's analysis.
Mud's sieved and drained from pewter into gold.
Conjectural infinity's outdone
By engineering, light and hydrous fact,
A waterfront that rises fold by fold
Into the stars beyond the last of stone,
A city's elements, local, exact.

Apples

I eat an apple, skin, core and pips,
And sleep at night the way a yokel sleeps
With thyme and borage in my palliasse,
Lavender pillows in the house of grass.

Apples of Portnauld, scarlet, round and good,
Ripened, come autumn, into savoury
Pleasures. I picked, then chewed in solitude
Behind the crumbling wall, out of the way.

I don't know why I should remember this –
Perhaps the pippin was enough to do it
With its hard flesh, delicious, bitten kiss.
I sit tonight and it is very quiet.

Broughty Ferry

Under the eaves, Elysian icicles
Taper towards stilled drips. In my garden
A naked birch looks lacquered by a hand
Expert in Christmas things or fairyland
Translations. Clever frost has hardened lace

On spiderwebs and shrubs. It has blinded glass
All over the planthouse, and spelled a rose
Into a shuttered bud.

On Broughty Ferry's mansioned slopes, houses
Address the sun I set my eye by, stepping
Through wintry trees, and there's an hour to go
Before the roselight comes to fill the sky.
Yesterday's money celebrates its stone
With watery, cold, imperial
Throwbacks to somewhere else, a hesitant
Refrigerated Orient.

I came home through the Country Bus Station
Eager for half-past-one and views from Fife.
A winey down-and-out, his poly bag
No bundle for a shouldered stick, outstared
Distaste and sentiment, a holly sprig
Defiant in his cap of weathered tweed.
A well-dressed mother with her hand-held son
Resented being there and looked away.

A simpleton went through a dance routine
Shuffling on the cold tiles of the alcove,
Pulling the faces of a mind content
With suffering's low comedy.
A one-legged pigeon hopped between the queues
With messages from Orphic pauperdom.
Cherubic sparrows huddled in their rags.
Policewomen struggled with a runaway.

Inspectors helped a blind man on a bus,
Then when their backs were turned, got off again,
Chasing white probes with thirst or memory.
Young men and women swaggered on the platform,

Loitering, discontent and ghetto-blasting.
Old women, frightened by the depot's
Aroma'd roar, fingered their counted change
Or checked their travel passes, passports home.

My comfortable, mind-aggrandized visions
Melt in the light and then my eyes play tricks
Or beauty tricks my eyes into conceit:
I won't disfigure loveliness I see
With an avoidance of its politics.
Although the silvered rust of docken seed
Shows it has none, nor whitened, brittle grass,
That isn't true of Broughty Ferry's stone,

Improved by roselight's neutral flawlessness,
Dismissing what I think of what I see
Into a stunned perfection, remote,
Depopulated and complacent.
I think of incomes and prosperity.
It comes to Wednesday's rhymed phrase
Holding together versions of events,
Significance that beauty can't erase.

Here and There

'Everybody's got to be somewhere.'
Woody Allen

You say it's mad to love this east-coast weather –
I'll praise it, though, and claim its subtle light's
Perfect for places that abut on water
Where swans on tidal aviaries preen their whites.
You whisper in the south that even the rain
Wins my affection, and I won't deny it,

Watching it drench my intimate domain:
I love the rain and winds that magnify it.
The evening's paper-boy goes round the doors
At his hour of November when the day's
Closing in goose-cries and the sycamores
Darken to silhouettes by darker hedges –

I love that too. *'Provincial'*, you describe
Devotion's minutes as the seasons shift
On the planet: I suppose your diatribe
Last week was meant to undercut the uplift
Boundaries give me, witnessed from the brae
Recording weather-signs and what birds pass
Across the year. More like a world, I'd say,
Infinite, curious, sky, sea and grass
In natural minutiae that bind
Body to lifetimes that we all inhabit.
So spin your globe: Tayport is Trebizond
As easily as a regenerate

Country in which to reconstruct a self
From local water, timber, light and earth,
Drawing the line (this might please you) at golf
Or watersports on a sub-Arctic Firth.
It matters where you cast your only shadow,
And that's my answer to, *'Why did you choose
Grey northland as your smalltown El Dorado?
You've literature and a career to lose ...'*
It isn't *always* grey. And what is grey?
A colour like the others, snubbed by smart
Depressives who can't stroll an estuary
Without its scope of sky bleaching their hearts.

'... You'll twist your art on the parochial lie.'
I love the barbed hush in the holly tree.
'An inner émigré, you'll versify,
Not write. You'll turn your back on history.'
Old friend, you're good for me, but what I want's
Not what your southern bigotry suspects.
Here on imagination's waterfronts
It's even simpler: fidelity directs
Love to its place, the eye to what it sees
And who we live with, and the *whys* and *whens*
That follow *ifs* and *buts*, as, on our knees,
We hope for spirit and intelligence.

Turbulence reaches here: the RAF
Loosens the earwax – so, not paradise
Unless you're awkward, Tory, daft or deaf
Or dealing in destruction's merchandise.
I hold my infant son at the window.
Look, there's the blue; I show him sky and the leaf
On the puddle. What does a baby know
Of the hazardous world? An acrid *if*
Diseases happiness, the damned *perhaps*
Perfected by the uniforms of State.
Our sunlit roofs look nothing on their maps
Other than pulverable stone and slate.

A ferry town, a place to cross from ... Verse
Enjoys connections: fugitive Macduff
Escaped Macbeth by it. Lacking his purse,
He paid in bread – The Ferry of the Loaf...
'Ferries? Fairies! That's medieval farce!'
The wizard, Michael Scot, was born near here...
'I might have guessed you'd more like that, and worse...'
... Alchemist, polymath, astrologer

[184]

To the Holy Roman Empire; Tayport's son
Mastered all knowledge, too controversial
For Dante who invented his damnation
In the *Inferno*. 'Tayport Man in Hell,'

They'd say in the *Fife Herald* – 'Sorcerer
From Tayport Slandered byTuscan Poet.'
'*Worse than parochial! Literature
Ought to be everywhere ...*' Friend, I know that;
It's why I'm here. My accent feels at home
In the grocer's and in Tentsmuir Forest.
Without a Scottish voice, its monostome
Dictionary, I'm a contortionist –
Tongue, teeth and larynx swallowing an R's
Frog-croak and spittle, social agility,
Its range of fraudulence and repertoires
Disguising place and nationality.

'*What's this about Tayport's centenary?
I never thought you'd prime a parish pump.*'
Not me. Who's said I have? '*It's scenery
You're there for.*' No, it isn't. '*Mugwump!*'
You're wrong again, old friend. Your Englishness
Misleads you into Albionic pride,
Westminstered mockery and prejudice –
You're the provincial, an undignified
Anachronism. The Pax Britannica's
Dismissed, a second-rate Byzantium,
Self-plundered inner empire's Age of Brass.
No houseroom's left in the imperial slum.

And as for scenery, what's wrong with love's
Preferred country, the light, water and sky
Around a town, centennial removes

From time? – The universe within the eye,
Cosmogyny, not parish-governed stars
Cultured above the Tay, but seen from here
When late-night amateur philosophers
Puzzle the substance of their hemisphere.
Time, space and yours truly: all men deserve
Somewhere, if only that, fruition's place,
Quotidian but extra, on a curve
That's capable of upwards into grace,

Eccentric elegance, the personal life
Sharing its ordinariness of days
With speculative spirit which is midwife
To nation, intellect and poetry's
Occurrence. *'You're looking for a chance to wear*
A three-piece suit in tweeds with heavy brogues,
Rehearsing presbyterian despair
On a shoreline, in Reithean monologues.'
So what, if I talk to myself in the woods?
'Perverse retreat into the safe and small
Suggests fake self-denial.' These latitudes
Enlarge me, comfort me, and make me whole.

'No, you're evasive, knowing it might be wrong
To hedge ambition into quietude
That serves a lowered will with local song,
Beachcombing an iambic neighbourhood.'
It serves my loyalty. It serves increase.
I'll keep no secrets from you: it serves love;
It serves responsibility and caprice.
Damn all careers; I'd rather *be* than *have.*
'You mean, it serves you right?' I hope so, friend.
Pay me a visit and we'll drink to life

One evening when the light and water blend
On the conjectural points of coastal Fife.

Come by the backroads with a sense of time.
Come like Edward Thomas on a holiday
In search of passages of wild-flowered rhyme
No Scot or Irishman would dare betray.
Now, though, I'm going out to the black twigs,
Shy waterbuds reflecting as they drop
To the neighbourly, where the good ground swigs
Any libation from its earthen cup.
Scottishness, if you say so; but I see
Plurals and distances in voiceless wet
Enough to harbour all my history
Inside a house protected from regret.

December's Door
in memoriam Philip Larkin

I kept a church leaf, wishing it were blossom.
    Hull's undressed roadside sycamores
Waded through brittle drifts from Cottingham
    To Newland Park, the still striders.
That leaf still marks my place, but it was worn
    Before I put it there; now dust
Dirties the page, and sinews, strong as thorn,
    Impress the paper's softer crust,
Fragments hanging from them, leaves of a leaf
    Preserved into a second autumn.
Afterwards' keepsake, its botanic grief
    Crumbles in death's *ad infinitum*.

A rudimentary, unclouded sky:
    That day in Hull, your funeral,
I watched rubescent figments vitrify
    On library windows, unreal
Emblems of warehoused English literature
    On the Fifth Floor, and saw again –
When I was in my twenties, I worked there –
    Hull's hazily Utopian green
Purpled and pinkened in a luminous
    Record of seasons. Long straight roads
Reached out across nocturnal Holderness,
    The sea and the visitless woods.

A leaf-marked book aches on my windowsill.
    Straw gold and central green were there
A year ago, but book-locked winterkill
    Disfigured them in printed air.
In a closed shadow, opened now, a door
    Into December's estuary
Beneath a wigged moon, it honeys the floor
    To starry oak, reflected Tay.
Geese draw their audible, Siberian bow
    Over the moon and Buddon Ness,
And now I can't repay the debt I owe,
    A withered leaf, a dry distress.

Sorrow's vernacular, its minimum,
    A leaf brought in on someone's shoe
Gatecrashed the church in muffled Cottingham,
    Being's late gift, its secret value
A matter of downtrodden poetry,
    Diminutive, and brought to this
By luck of lyric and an unknown tree.
    A passer-by was bound to notice

Crisp leaves at work when everyone had gone,
    Some fricative on paving-stones
As others flecked a winter-wrinkled lawn,
    Remote, unswept oblivions.

Winkie
'We also serve'

GIVE ME GOOD PIGEONS!
    You pose in your glass case
    Putting a brave face on your taxidermed
    Municipal afterlife.
Close by you, Winkie, is a photograph,
A bomber's aircrew snapped in the Second War.
You were their mascot and survival kit.
    Click-click went their tongues;
    And *Winkie-Winkie* they sang
Pressing titbits through the wooden bars
On leather and vibrating fingers.
Winkie-Winkie chirped the goggled men.

Over Norway, its fuselage and wings on fire,
The bomber droned down to the sea,
    Flames sizzling in sleet
    As frantic signals pinged
Against deaf radio ears in nowhere.

Cupped hands released you from a rubber boat.
    Miniature of instinct,
    Dedicated one, your stuffed breast swells
    With pride in your only nature!

GIVE ME GOOD PIGEONS!
Their *chuck-chuck-chuck's*
A thwarted cooing from the woods
Haunting city squares
Named for dimwits and dignitaries
With old bucolic neighbourhoods,
Fife, Gowrie and the Mearns.
Whether as spy-birds on a sneaky errand
Bearing a snip of microfilm for eyes
Devoted to secrecy, released by a hand
Clandestinely over a window-sill in Warsaw,
Or with the gentler mail of love, birth and death
Winged over the suburbs and snipers from
The besieged city – see the rifle, the Prussian eye
Point through the foliage round the gardened villas –
You are liberty's bird,
Unstreamlined and civilian,
With the guts and stamina of a taxpayer
And behind you the solidarity of your species,
The Univeresal Union of Pigeons.

Your mission doesn't matter
Nor what unvisa'd coasts
You cross on your postal expeditions,
Nor the direction you take, or whatever
Nationality is claimed for the forests below
Or who pretends to own the air and seasons
And the pronunciation of rivers and mountains.
The blame is not yours –
Docile legionary,
Warrior bearing words,
Beloved of the Intelligence Services'
Eccentric dogsbodies,
Dovecote attendants

In the obscurest ministerial spires
With their bowls and jugs, their bags of maize
For kept cushats, *pigeons voyageurs*, homers,
Birds of the cloak-and-dagger cryptography.

An imprisoned lover turns on his stinking straw
And a dove at the window chortles.
A letter is read to the sound of cooing.

I do not like the big brave boasts of war.
   GIVE ME GOOD PIGEONS! –
A very large number of Great Commoners
Built like Nye Bevan or Gambetta.

   Winkie read his charts
On his table of instinct, and found the Tay's dent
   On the planet of places.
   A perfect rescue – saved by a bird
   Homing down to Carnoustie.

Bird of X-marks-the-spot
Bird of the ringed foot, married to the miles
Bird of human purpose but immune to guilt
Bearer of tidings and long-distance billet-doux
Reports of troop movements, the planned assassination
Scorner of moats, guard towers and jammed radio
Dove that to a hand in Babylon
Brought more news of the strange horsemen
And bird that to Chaucerian casements brought
Melodious greetings to the heartsick Lady
Bird of the allotments, bird of the long race
Hand-held bird, heartbeat in gentle hands
Olympic bird, love-bird, bird of the peace
Dove of the Annunciation, forerunner of Christ
Bird of the strange beam and the beautful lily

Mendicant bird, begging around footwear
With your jabbing head, your hungry, urban strut

FLY, WINKIE, FLY!

Muir's Ledgers

Men hurry in a scuff of studs down cobbled wynds,
Heads bent in a dark morning, blowing on their hands.
The Firth-side farms are fleeing from the winter salts;
Defrosting hammers, skin and fire on nuts and bolts
Elaborate their work-noise in the river's yards.
From their Italianated villas, river-lords
Look out on blueing mountains and relaxing yachts;
Self-made propriety's bucked up in morning suits.
Left angry wives, with bairns, in smells of breakfast,
Are unaware the winter light is colourist,
Although kimono'd wives, whose children are at school
In England, buy pictures from Peploe, Hunter and Cadell.
Now Edwin Muir walks from the tram to be a clerk
In Renfrew where the river flows like liquid work
Past Lobnitz's, a shipyard where his writing fills
Commercial ledgers with lists of materials.
Doves on a ledge, a corner of town hall baronial,
Remind him of the future life he'll live in verses
Which, one day, he'll write, in towns other than this.

A House in the Country

'O God! I could be bounded in a nut-shell, and count myself
a king of infinite space, were it not that I have bad dreams.
                                                    Hamlet

Not Scotland. The colour of the stone
Remembers somewhere *sur Vézère*
Or Tuscany, the Serchio's watertone
Italianate among the cocklebur.

Unopened years burst loose, an iron gate
Inched on its hindered arc, its squeak
Increasing as my bodyweight
Crushes its rust through cry to scream and shriek.

A sore path, and illegible:
Its arrow-headed thorns nip legs and hands –
Red-beaded bracelets and a scratched standstill
Waist-deep in brambled reprimands.

The door's decayed and locked: flaked paint and rust,
Negative timbers on which wood-weeds cling,
One in flower. A doorpost
Crumbles on toe-touch, shuddering.

A kick would smash this door.
I look around and wonder where I am,
Hearing my blood percuss, the red drummer,
Then find a key cold on my sweating palm.

Webs lace the narrow hall. Floorboards protest
At the weight of my shadow, disgruntled
Cries that release an insect ghost,
Digested flies on a transparent scaffold.

A joist gives on my afterstep. Wood quits
Its fastenings. House-sounds reverberate
In a grey resonance as powdery minutes
Clamour for quiet and then hesitate

On their hazards, blinking in light
Shuttered until now, sneaking
Through keyholes, under doors, off-white
On plaster puddles, the whole house creaking.

A sitting room's dust-sheeted furniture
Dwells on its family thoughts in indoor silence,
The frequency on which its spiders hear
Their lives and predatory conversations

Passing down lifetimes, polyphonic with
Remembered chit-chat or a chair's
Collected memories. Piano breath
Withdraws into its contemplated quavers.

Books and a desk; a jacket's shape
Transforms a chair into a studious shrug,
An amputated, headless stoop
Mouthing a dusty monologue,

Pulling the darkness down
As seasons, politics and swallows pass
And natural and human transformation
Recur on dusty window-glass.

In swirls of air and daylight alien
To it, reluctantly, the room confronts
Sky, wind and summer's herbal rain,
Noise, light and celebrants.

A grey globe ponders on its plinth,
A sphere within a varnished O's embrace
Hugging the planetary labyrinth,
Its cuddled continents all out of place.

Webs fold and curdle in the sunlit wind's
Expulsion of the shadows, and a man
Appears from nowhere or the mind's
Liberty to be more than one.

I am nowhere, everywhere and past
In a house in a country I do not know
A stone clock on the mantel grinds to dust
Minutes that were lifetimes long ago

'No, not that door,'
He says. 'Look at your mirrored face.
You'll learn you've visited that room before
In other houses in another place.

'Reality's the ghost
Stalking your privacy and footsteps
With minstrelsies. Your innermost
Identity eavesdrops

'On what it does and where it goes with you
Among the flowers and clocks, perfidy, faith,
The groves of rooms that utter you
Beyond the physical and into death.'

And then he says again: 'No, not that door.'
Skeletal alphabets
Drop from their bookshelves to the rubbled floor,
Trash *videlicets*

Dismembered from their etymologies,
Words and the shards of an unspoken word,
Lost mouths and dumb debris
Emaciated and disordered.

Hereafter's solitary, rooted to
His captive afterlife disturbed by me,
He spins his globe, and dust-clouds clear to blue
Oceans, green continents and history.

Imagined stranger, I am in your house
By ways of sleep and owls, and you know why
The door you guard's the door I have to choose
Before my cowardice becomes a lie.

A Snow-walk

What's haunting what, the birchwood or the snow?
It feels too European – this high, barbed fence,
A dog barking, a shot, and the sub-zero
Mid-winter rippled by a mortal cadence.

The water-tower near McGregor's house
Rejects its hurtful simile and slips
Behind the blizzard's curtain – ominous,
Re-memoried or rumoured guardianships.

White shelves on cypresses; and history's
Gaunt silver on a feathered crucifix –
A hawk nailed by its wings, a predatory
Snow-narrative retold in dead athletics.

Large tree-stumps, scattered through a chain-sawed wood,
Metamorphose to dust-cloth'd furniture,
Closed forest rooms, palatial solitude,
Iced armchairs and a branch-hung chandelier.

That fence again; a sign – *Guard Dogs Patrolling*.
Embedded in the snow, low huts appear,
A disused railway line, the shed for coaling,
A toppled goods van and a snow-filled brazier.

Home feels a life away and not an hour
Along the length of an industrial fence,
By friendly holdings and a water-tower
Robbed of simplicity and innocence.

Jig of the Week No. 21

Under optimum conditions – the room quiet
In fireglow, rain lashing on nocturnal glass –
I start an old American puzzle.
It smells like my Webster's dictionary;
It reminds me of the lesson in Latin
Translating Lincoln's *Gettysburg Address*
Into my Ciceronian of errors.
On junior versions of wet, wintry nights
Around Christmas, I tried to be patient,
A jigsaw on a white enamel tray
Encouraging pictorial wanderlust –
My father's ear close to the wireless set's
Hummed murmuring of Cold War '49,
My mother sewing, my brother fast asleep.
Posed by the artist in a daze of stunned
Courage, a wounded man waves in the paint,

A salutation from a grassy foreground.
Here is a piece of sky; this one's a hoof.
I give a man his legs, then rummage for
A clue of horse, a clump of grass. Slaughter's
Perfectionists, the North Virginian troops
March through the woods of Pennsylvania
Intent on orders and aesthetic war.
Omniscient history makes good puzzles:
This one is *Pickett's Charge at Gettysburg*.
Jigsaw research – whose side was Pickett on?
I look him up, then file a book away.
The man who painted this supported Blue;
My mind and fingers soldier with the Grey.
Three hundred fragments of American
Cardboard carnage! This old Bostonian box
Crossed the Atlantic sixty years ago;
Thousands went all over the United States
Shipped by the Universal Distribution Company.
A segment finishes the Stars and Stripes
Carried before blue-trousered infantry.
A dozen pieces, more or less the same,
Assemble shell bursts, foliage and sky,
Turquoise and pink, a summer's afternoon
On Cemetery Ridge, the Butcher's Bill
Extortionate in fact but not in paint –
Invoices brought at night, slipped under doors.
A painter oiled his military bias,
For a good price, and then his work became
A reproduction of a reproduction
Issued in multiples, mail-ordered
All over childhood to the merry puzzlers.
You can open old wounds like a box,
That slow knitting of pictures and glory

In Tennessee and Massachusetts.
I hold an inch of space, the missing piece,
The notional and beautiful republic
Expressing what was fought for and who died,
'The last full measure of devotion . . .'
– Put hats on heads, place heads on fallen men
And resurrect the dead, the broken wheels:
A finished puzzle ends up in a dream,
A subterranean, consecrated picnic,
A hand waving in the fraternal paint.

In the 1950s

The Courier was full of it. A whole page
Described the opening of the new transmitter,
Those who were there, how they were dressed, and who
Got up to speak and what they talked about.
He read it out to me, and I could tell
From his pauses, as I stood with my duster,
That soon we'd have one in our living room.
I could see myself cleaning it, wiping the screen,
Knowing the corner where I'd put the set
To best advantage, where he would sit, where I
Would sit, moving the chairs a few feet round
Away from the fire.
                    I missed the cinema.
Each Sunday I read out what was on that week,
And if he showed an interest, I'd learned
How he'd forget; or if one had a star
Or story that I knew he'd want to see,
He'd point out how it was too far away
With the last bus back at seven, his work

Such that he never had a Saturday
To himself, and the Roxy shut on Sundays.

I coaxed his willingness until I felt
A screenlight falling on our furniture;
And as he read out what the programmes were
I thought of how the wireless missed me out
As we sat, he listening or seeming to,
Me with my sewing as the fire collapsed
Down on its woody ash, and bedtime chimed
Its moment on the wedding-present clock.
Above the comedies, applause and news,
That world of people laughing in London,
I listened without listening and sewed.

It wasn't that we easily afforded one
Or that he had the sort of pride which made him
Pushy to buy the first set in our district.
Old Struthers ducked, trying to dodge the custard
Tossed by a funnyman in the slapstick.
'Nation', he quoted, 'shall speak peace unto nation.'
It was worth it, to see Anderson jealous –
His wife forbade it as the Devil's gadget –
With three tractors, a new car every year.
After that first few weeks of visitors
Eating my scones, my cherry cake and biscuits,
We sat in the dark, adjusting the light
By lamps and curtains ... Contrast, Brightness,
The Vertical and Horizontal Holds:
He read the handbook like his *Scottish Farmer*.
I put my sewing down for a whole month.
We talked again, always of what we watched,
In that half hour of the cooling set.
His rural body leaned towards the screen

As if his promised 'window on the world'
Yielded too small a square of it, or gave
Too much of life beyond the one he lived.
And half the time his mouth hung open on
A wonder or resentment as he prowled
The screen, his eyes on all fours, watching, fooled
And frightened by those toffs 'in town tonight'.
Names that he couldn't talk to were his masters.
'Some day,' he said 'I'll take us both to London.'
Soon there were aerials on other roofs.
Each time I saw the van from the Clydesdale
I felt a little less alone
On summer evenings with the curtains drawn.
Then everybody had one. My husband watched
The War at Sea, and then *War in the Air*;
He brought two Irish workmen once, to watch
A match: they sat with their caps on their knees.

I watched the children's shows, and wept for me –
That puppet on the top of the piano!
After these years of news and Michelmore,
Of Gilbert Harding and the Weatherman,
I'd look south thinking that I knew the world
As I pegged my washing up against the wind.
And then the Sixties, the Seventies, changes
Our entertainment half-prepared us for,
New houses, each with its aerial
From the day it was built, supermarkets,
The Motorway and the Industrial Estate:
He looked at them and felt responsible.

Now, in The Home, I seek The Quiet Room,
Finding my friends there with their whist and wool.
It is so hard to be alone and quiet

These days, even here, where many are dying;
But sometimes, after reading, I go down
To watch the late-night widowers and widows,
Their papers folded at The Viewer's Page.
'We never see you in the TV Lounge.'
'No. No,' I say. 'I pick my programmes now.'

The War in the Congo

A man in a bar in Glasgow told me of how
He'd served with the Irish Army in the Congo
Under the flag of the United Nations.
'It was hot,' he told me, 'hot, and equatorial.'

They passed through a deserted and dog-ridden town.
They passed a house that had been blown up.
An arm, with a hand, rose between blasted breeze-blocks.
In the black hand was an envelope, between fingers and thumb.

The Irish soldier looked at the hand and its letter.
Cement dust scabbed the blood on the arm.
He tore a corner off the envelope, removing the stamp,
Which he sent to his nephew in Howth, in Ireland.

In reply to what my companion asked him,
The soldier said it wasn't right to read a stranger's mail.
There was no one about in the little town, other than
Dogs and birds, and the arm and its hand, like a cleft stick.

He didn't say if it was the hand of a man or a woman
In which the letter was held, between fingers and thumb.
It was the arm of black Anon, of Africa,
Holding a letter, just received or unsent.

What concerns me is the soldier's nephew in Howth
Holding the piece of envelope with tweezers
Over the spout of a steaming kettle, and the stamp,
Renewed and drying between sheets of blotting-paper.

Philately of foreign wars is a boy in Howth
Licking a transparent hinge, and mounting a stamp
In his album, hot, hot and equatorial,
That innocent know-nothing stamp, lonesome in history.

Did he or she read it, that letter? Who wrote it? Who sent it?
So many stamps, and stamps from many countries,
And boys saying to their uncles and elder brothers,
'Remember, when you get there, to send me their stamps.'

4/4

in memoriam John Brogan

There was that night at pleasant Kate's
When you beat out your boogie'd bars
Among the bow-tied advocates
Swaying like minor characters
Of the Enlightenment, their laws
Dismantled by your drag and pause.
Your left hand's rhythmic boom and walk
Shivered the porcelain and crushed
Twelve strokes of midnight on the clock.
Even the chatterboxes hushed.
Like a young Hoagy Carmichael –
Thinking, smoking, drinking, sociable –
You used to stare out through your fug
With that half-smile of early wisdom,
Part intellectual, part rogue,

Pro life and *anti* tedium.
Here's to your memory, Jack,
Leaning into a whispered joke
Or a conspiracy against
Conservatives and sundry shits
Whose pranks or phoniness incensed
Distrust of the patriciates.
And here's to yesterday's State Bar
And to the socialism of pleasure;
Here's to that half-cut afternoon
Jamming at Jimmy's in Rutherglen
Until my beat-up tenor sax
Spat springs and pads, giving it max,
When Lithuania's silver flute
Whistled its lyric absolute.
Bohemians with haircuts, glass
In hand, the decent working-class
Created us for politics
In which we talked but couldn't lead,
Read poetry, played jazz instead,
Our undeclared republic's
Ferocity discussed and shelved
As notional and unresolved.
Strange how we served the cause of books:
Knowledge, a pike to stand behind
At barricades of love and mind –
Read this, and contradict the crooks!
This toast's to our librarianship –
I catalogue each taste and sip.
A drink, too, for our generation's
Withered ideals, that dwindled sense,
Sold out, tormented innocence
And salaried impatience.

So here's to booze's brotherhood
Puking on Ballageich Hill.
It didn't do us any good,
But what the hell, Jack, what the hell.

Maggie's Corner

Round and round, caught in a loop of film,
I walk ahead of who and where I am.
I turn the corner named for Maggie Earl.
The same old postbox reddens on her wall.

When Maggie ran Inchinnan's corner shop
Its stewed light was the shade of tinkers' tea.
Her corner keeps her name. It won't give up.
It smells of sweet-shop sugared memory.

Nostalgia's a bam. Distrust its stink.
Four decades old, and still that powerful dream
Pervades the mental twilight with its pink
Light-puddles on a rural housing-scheme.

I think of calls made from the corner's kiosk.
'Press *Button B*' and it's a wintry dusk.
A weathered, retrospective second-sight
Will see me catch the front-road bus tonight

With three half-crowns, a folded ten-bob note,
To buy the evening for a girl and me.
Here, everywhere, forethought and afterthought,
Nowhere and nothing's what I think I see,

Or what I thought I thought, or saw, no if
Or but about it, just the world I'm in.
My heart beats back and forth across a life
Bearing its spoon of blood like medicine.

Running the East Wind

It runs ahead of me on gaseous muscle.
It is the steep hill within me,
Planning my exhaustion.
Sleet and hail goad me like commissars.

It comes airmail from Murmansk
Leaving behind its scent of reindeer,
Its Lapp and Scandinavian accents,
Dropping its cold swords in the North Sea.

I do this for my health's sake
And because I used to like it, not for
Siberian sport, a spectral braggart
Showing off in its icy gymnasium.

A Syrian auxiliary felt this wind
On what was left of his sun-tan.
He listened to its half-Arctic jokes
Then slew the prisoners.

The Ice Queen is laughing at
My goose-bumps, my acidic saliva.
This wind is her regiment of snow-cossacks.
Wet life huddles in the hedgerows.

Coniferous Tentsmuir whistles in its forest.
I surrender, and the wind turns into swift urchins
Begging handouts from my breath.
They are stripping my lungs.

It turns again and pushes me like a pram.
It runs its fingers through my hair
Bearing me home on its transparent vehicles,
On its millions of glassy wheels.

In-flight Entertainment

Time lets its scientific minutes drop
On the Australian emptiness, a brown
Rugged geology where clocks are baked
In God's kiln, earthenware timepieces
Computing natural spans of insect life
Anticlockwise. Marginal nature gets by
Where there's no one to go for a walk with
And the first and last footprints slid under
Into deserted time and dry grottoes
Yesterday or millennia ago,
It makes no difference. That town beneath us,
Without buildings, fencing or municipality,
Might be the place called Nevermore, a dry
Republic ruled by solar plutocrats.
Some clown crossed it on camelback, others
Discovered the dotted line of their hot trek
Staggering over the unwritten map
Into a parched waterhole, imagining
Their own bones posed as they would leave them,
Deliberate, heroic litter,

Dissolving into horror, then into spirit.
So, better to sit up straight, back to a rock,
And hope for dignity in the annals,
A winged shadow casting its event of shade
To the cries of lost nomads and explorers.
    At thirty thousand feet, it's all go now
In our flying cinema. Earphones bring me
Time whiled away in in-flight entertainment.
I choose the channel called Heavenly Choirs
In the programme, but I'm in the wrong mood
For celestial flutes and the twanged God-harp
Concertos commissioned by the airline.
An Indonesian turbulence brings on
Spontaneous fidgeting with seat-belt buckles,
Ashtrays, and, in one case, a rosary.
It's as anxious as disaster's soundtrack.
My drink rumbas across its trembling tray.
Schooners on the Conradian sea and Dutch
East Indiamen race for the sheltered bays
Tiny under volcanoes, spice-bundles tied
In palm-roofed warehouses by windy wharfs.
Our big bird flutters its mineral feathers
Going down by invisible staircases
Through tropical rain, our slow descent driven
Straight to the shopkeepers of Singapore
And the days when I clerked for Stamford Raffles
In his turbanned garrison, mastering
Malay and opportunities of The Straits.
This airport doesn't feel like terra firma,
More like a space station, a half-way house
Between the stars and British history.
    Dark now, all the way to London, and sleep
Goes by me on its glass sails, not stopping

Throughout these pages of our *bon voyage*.
Over the Bay of Bengal, I walk down
Aromatic corridors, and India dozes
Beneath three hundred tons of rapid weight
And people crossing the world in three bounds.
I can see nothing but sacred darkness
On the underside of the wind, a glow
Where cloudy light describes a multitude
Dreaming in its city, its electric bowl.
I fall into a cultured quarter-sleep,
One eye half-open like a crocodile's.
Fictitious light squirms on the movie screen
But absentmindedness narrates another tale.
Reality's make-believe, and that's its point:
I've dreamt myself into mistaken times,
Not where I am, but all over the place.
The present's just as bad – the clock's going back,
But everyone's fixed to biological forwards.
Their destiny, like mine, is to grow old
As fate, or pilot error, has it, weather,
Metal fatigue, or ghostly horsemen from
The Mogul Empire, riding the stratosphere.
We're all travelling from the twenty-ninth
To the twenty-eighth, still living in
Yesterday, which takes us to Bahrain,
Where I have never been before. Pirates
On perilous star-dhows swing from the moon's
Islamic sickle, serious, cut-throat Sinbads.
 High over Babylon and Nineveh,
Ancient astronomers observe our lights;
Soothsayers with the troops of Alexander
Read our high thunder as a sacred omen.
I remember my classics teacher saying,

'Ah, yes, the Hittites ... Who were the Hittites, boy?'
And there they are, the Hittites, one and all,
To say nothing of Midas, Mithridates,
Phrygia, Pontus and the satrapies
In Europe's Asian antithesis.
Where else should turn up next on my agenda
If not Byzantium outlined in neon
Advertisements, Marmora, Bosphorus?
Now that we're all awake, I hear a fool
Refer to down-below as Istanbul.
Where has he been for these past thousand years?
   Miletus once was mighty, long ago.
I drag an adage over the Roman Empire,
Its winter vineyards, olive groves and highways,
Nocturnal autobahns, palatinates.
Night-lights in the European bedroom yield
To dawn and England in November.
Stiff knees and sleeplessness: I saw no God
In my internal flying-time throughout
These indoor hours at mighty altitude.
Those on the other wing can see the Thames,
Westminster foggy and Big Ben at seven.
Change terminals, change planes, process the bags,
This London never could be north enough
For me and who I love and travel with
And who has slept through half of geography.

The Departures of Friends in Childhood

With optimism at the thrill of it –
The rarity of a taxi, suitcases stowed
On the floorboards and the furniture sold –
They drove through green shadows at the ends of lanes
To where-you-will in every New-Found-Land,
Ontario, North Island, New South Wales.
And always our mothers would say, 'Give them
Something of yours, the thing you love best' –
An envied marble, the left-handed boxing glove –
Knowing that their mothers would say the same –
A triangular stamp, a lightweight Egyptian piastre;
And anyone with cash or curiosity
Attended the auctions of gardening tools,
Bicycles, wireless sets and the forlorn shoes.
Boys would fight for the last time and shake hands,
Our clumsily affectionate farewells!
'Goodbye,' girls said to each other, 'Goodbye.'
At the exchange of gifts, at tea-parties
Invented out of rationed tea and sugar,
There seemed the promise of love to others
Waiting for them in the lands of the atlas.
In a place they wouldn't recognize, the wind
In the remaining tree cries in its wisdom,
Its leaves repeating the summer noise for For Ever
To names I can't remember as I listen to
Emigrant songs, the sundered families.
One butterfly where once there were so many.

The Dark Crossroads

Its small door asks its customers to stoop.
   Inside, a redesigned antiquity
Reproaches strangers entering to quench
   A travel-thirst or drouth of field-labour.
No rural innocents: ale-tinted light
   Died long ago behind the panelling
And that hand-painted sign above the door –
   The licensee's name drawn in Georgian cursive –
Fakes yesteryear as neatly as tankards
   Hooked in commemorative pewter rows.
Horse-brasses, warming-pans, foxed sporting prints,
   Yeomanry carbines crossed above the hearth,
Depict quondam society, preserved
   In the shadows of low-ceilinged aforetime,
Sweat's trinketry and souvenirs of servants,
   Billhooks of hedgers, rural militia's
Sabres, and a framed box of brass buttons.
   Men in blazers, hacking jackets, cravats,
Tweeds, suede shoes and cavalry twill trousers,
   Preside with gin, the diehards of opinions
Made in this place. A regimental tie
   Addresses me and tries to weigh my mind
Through sockets of its death's head insignias.
   The publican is Wing Commander X
Standing beside two sleeping Dobermanns.
   Five words have uttered who I am and where
I come from, like a paragraph: scoundrels,
   Tenements, drunkenness, their false Scotland.
You don't speak back in this company, unless
   You want to feel imaginary rope
Around your neck at the dream-gallows

Carpentered quickly by a psychopath
Sanctioned by his satanic magistrates.
   I am an uppity Jock without valour,
Not lacking, though, in discretion, here,
   Where cavaliers bluster over thinned spirits
With fossilized, sinister gaiety.
   I find a snug corner. A pint of beer
Helps me to while away an English hour
   Until the bus that starts my journey home
Arrives nearby, at a stop where a man
   Sits on a stone with his newspaper, flask
And sandwiches, a woman with a caged hen
   Observing sixty minutes dwindle on
Her wristwatch, hidden by a tight, tugged sleeve.
   I picture what it looks like from outside –
The thatch, the whitewash and the mullioned windows
   Negotiating eighteenth-century trust,
A rendezvous with ordered permanence,
   As they might see it, crowded at the bar,
Turning to look at me. One man goes through
   His repertoire of 'Scotsmen I have known'.
I'm meant to hear. The calculated voice
   Distributes mirth, rakish jocosity
Bred in the hearty schools of prejudice.
   'Their place,' I warn myself. 'Leave it alone.'
But I do this, this notional revenge,
   A necessary act of wickedness
As pride humps ire, of which I am not proud.
   History moves against us once again.
Voice-niggers and any-shade victims of skin
   Devise their slave revolts, indigenous
Dreams of the moss trooper, the righteous horseman.
   Disturbed by bad aggrandizement, theirs, mine –

Unwanted thoughts, but unaccountable –
    I stand in fine rain watching dust curdle.
When privileged disdain mounts its high horse,
    Testing the stirrups, the sabre's edge,
It's time to mount your own, hearing the note
    That gathers schiltrons to the wapinschaw,
Though these are words and obsolete signals
    Describing a defensive hate, bloodlust
Soured into ink, a library carnage.

An Address to Adolphe Sax in Heaven
For Ted Tarling

That your great gift to human ears
Offended purist connoisseurs
Might not be weird, but that's the word
They thought described the sound they heard.
Though Berlioz defended it
Most maestros reprehended it,
While Richard Wagner's saxophobics
Call for a mouthful of aerobics –
Rassenkreuzungsklangwerkzeuge.
Unrhymable! It's on its own,
Your 'instrument of hybrid tone'.
Bizet in his *L'Arlésienne* –
A sound like lyric Caliban –
Raised eyebrows as he lowered the tone
With solos for a saxophone.
Parisian social experts feared
The sound of sex was what they heard,
Melodic monsters, Minotaurs,
Breaking down their bedroom doors.

Its complicated *quidditas*
Prognosticated future jazz.
Not what you had in mind, *cher Sax*:
Concertos, not yackety-yaks,
Were more your forte. You would love
The alto one by Glazunov,
Ibert's, or Pierre Max Dubois's
Alto-harmonious noise.

   Bordellos and the regiments
Took greatly to your insruments.
Your lacquered cosmopolitans
Marched under hot, colonial suns,
And, in a room behind the bar
In Senegal or Côte d'Ivoire,
Melodies no conservatoire
Would ever countenance were played –
A Guadeloupan serenade
Or tune to set the heart astir
In an outpost of Madagascar.
Saharan saxophones! Annam
Transfigured by their 'priestly calm'!

   Think of the clarinets of France
With instrumental reverence! –
Hyacinthe Klosé and Leblanc,
Their breath, the fingerprints of song!
What better mouth as embouchure
Than one that says the word *amour*
Or when the clarinet's played low
Describes its sound as *chalumeau*?
Its 'simple system,' you, Sax, built–
So-called because it's difficult –
Found favour, but the laws of patent

Failed to discourage disputant
Competitors and plagiarists,
Invention's parasitic pests.
Not, though, your seven-belled trombone
That looked like the first telephone
Exchange, your *saxotromba's* freak
Ingenious *saxomblatarique*.
That elephantine hearing-aid
Ruptured and deafened those who played,
Or tried to, its enormous tones'
Almighty bass convulsions.

   Critical slander and derision
Postponed, but couldn't halt, your mission.
Low audiences applauded it
And your alumni in the pit
Stood up and wiped wine-sweaty brows
Taking their own, and their master's, bows.
You hoped for an orchestral glory;
Destiny wrote another story –
Hack-blowers in the Music Hall
And quick-march guardsmen in the Mall:
Ignored for a symphonic part
You put an *oompah* into art.
Ballroom, night-club and bawdy-house
Were futures for your posthumous
Discovery, the sound of feet
Dancing and tapping, indiscreet
Lyricism in the glowing smoke,
Venereal riffs and blue heartache
In Harlem or in *Barrowland*
Where half the orchestra were canned.
So, Sax, profanity's the fate

Your instruments negotiate
Through New Orleans to Buddy Tate
While saxophonic venery's
Libidinous communiqués
Disclose that St Cecilia's just
A woman when it comes to lust.
From Buffs and Garde Républicaine
To Charlie Parker and Coltrane!
Trumbauer, Hawkins, Chu and Bechet,
Lester, Sims and Cohn, and Wardell Gray,
Hodges, Webster, Rollins, Getz,
Lucky, Lockjaw, Dexter, Konitz
Brought oompah'd art to that fine pitch
Where music's an erotic itch
A fingernail's too blunt to scratch.

   Now look at you! From Aberdeen
To hamlets in the Argentine,
In Reykjavik and Birmingham,
Djakarta and Dar es Salaam,
High-stepping bands with majorettes
Play saxophones like martinets.
Your beggar with its inbuilt bowl's
Played in the cause of rock 'n' roll's
Electric millionaires, subfusc
Wee buggers with an urge to busk.

   A genius who invents a noise
Adds to the store of sonic toys
That *Homo ludens* in his wisdom
Accepts into his playful system.
Adolphe, once close to suicide,
Cher maître, take your place beside
Celebrity whose household name

Is dictionaried in its fame –
Derrick, the hangman, Heinz's beans,
Kellogg's cornflakes, Levi's jeans,
Ford of the cars and Louis Braille,
Freud, Epicurus, Chippendale,
Marx and the verse Petrarch devised,
Martini, and the pasteurized,
Newtonian Law, the arch of Goth,
Mackintosh's sea-proofed cloth,
And Wellington, he of the boot,
Good, optimistic King Canute,
Fabian's tactics, Mills' bomb,
The Midas touch, Brummell's aplomb,
Platonic love, Macadam's roads,
Several diseases, Pindar's odes,
Darwinianism, Cardigan,
And J. M. Barrie's Peter Pan.
From saxophone quartets by Strauss
On days off from the Opera House,
Or works by Milhaud and Ravel
Or Villa-Lobos in Brazil,
To Lester leaping in possessed
By his brass-belled iconoclast,
The sound we hear is yours, Adolphe,
Posterity, its howling wolf,
Time salivating on a reed
And fingering at breakneck speed.

The Country Kitchen

Madame Moulinier used to bring
Two rabbits a week, and two hens,
Still warm, but throttled. The kitchen's
Cutlery lacked a decent knife
But I did the best I could, wishing
There was an animal-opener
The equal in convenience
To what you'd use on a tin of beans.
Blood seeped from the blunt incisions.
Peeling each portion of their skins
The sounds were slight, but bad, and such
I had to shut my eyes and whistle.
It felt like pulling plasters off your leg –
The pain and noise of skin and hair.
The heads were worst of all –
The ears, the eyes, the little mouths.
Blood leaked from the drainpipe.
The house was bleeding.
As for the hens, I plucked feathers
Among the trees, beyond the house.
It took most of an afternoon.
It looked like an Indian massacre
When I'd finished – shattered head-dresses.
We cooked them in the big pot, *sauvage* –
Shallots, a muslin bag of herbs
Gathered from the neglected gardens.
Some of these herbs were weeds and grasses.
The dug garlic was green, but good.
So was the garnish of young chives.
On evening walks, I used to watch
The rabbits stare back from their hutch,

Wondering which bunny was next;
And the hens pecking white dirt – *dot, dot,*
And then the scare of a footstep.
I asked a peasant to sharpen my knife
On the stone he used for his scythe.
It made it easier, and it didn't –
My hand inside a hen's dead warmth,
Or slitting open the rabbits,
My wife saying, 'Keep the kidneys!' –
Amateur kitchen pathology.
So I said, 'I'm sick of rabbit;'
And, 'Another hen and I'll cluck!'
That village is announced by a fine sculpture.
A stone woman holds a stone child.
The woman's name is 'Abondance'.
I saw abundance all right:
In her stone bowls were stone vegetables,
Chiselled salads, a petrified artichoke.
I looked with envy at the walnut trees
Flourishing in botanical liberty.
The fishmonger's van was maritime,
Cold, dripping with melting ice,
An edible museum of the sea.
For nights on end I dreamt of close quarters
Boxed behind the nailed mesh,
Creeping backwards into furred heat,
Packed eyes and lettuce breath,
When ringed fingers dropped in
On a carnivorous visit.

from DANTE'S DRUM-KIT

Unlike Herons

An ageing President, an Earl, two Sirs,
Three Tory Scottish Office Ministers
(And let them guess which ministers they are)
And that dry, professorial character
An air-brushed Trotsky ghosted from the snap
A Moderator in a standing nap
Three surgeons round a corpse, surrealists
A huddle of emaciated priests
They seem to meditate on troubled sex
A synod of mudflat ecclesiastics
One like a well-known local plasterer
And one the double of a TV star
A feathered gourmet and a rich physician
A really awful Labour politician
Oh my, poor heron, what will you do-oo
These foolish things remind me of you-oo

Henry Petroski, *The Pencil. A History.*
Faber and Faber, £14.99

As something to write with a pencil is cute engineering.
For how did they manage to squeeze that cylindrical lead
Into the timber to make what we all find endearing
Even when marking exams in satirical red?

Professor Petroski knows more about pencils than anyone –
Discovery's digits, the fingers in tune with the mind,
Engineers sketching and dreaming of what can be done,
Transferring from paper to substance and something
    designed.

Far back in the Freudian distance the Latin word *penis*
Crops up in its origin, meaning 'a tiny wee tail' –
Royal Sovereign, Conté and Derwent, Faber and *Venus*:
Those monarchs of pencils are not quite exclusively male.

In Primary 1 they first taught us to write on a slate.
Diminutive Romans, we formed every letter by squeak;
Then that Day of the Pencils came round – worth the wait,
Though you sharpened them down to a stub in less than a
    week.

Pencil-box Kids, each with selections of colours and Hs and
    Bs;
Sweet-smelling shavings, the point that was sharp as a dart;
A 2B for tickling the back of a neck – and how she said
    'Please!';
Desk-top graffiti, the sums and the juvenile art.

Computerized reason and drafting are all very well
But you can't pick your nose with a screen, and keyboards
    won't do
When it comes to that cedary, graphite-and-alphabet smell,
While hardware and gadgetry leave you with nothing to
    chew.

Ball-points and fibretips search for invented perfection
But pencils are precious as paper is. Alloy and wood –
A pencil's a symbol of making; earth grants its affection
When what man gets up to with nature is useful and good.

Petroski puts pressure on more than the point of his pencil.
'Two cultures' are One in his book. Controversy dies:
Artists and scientists using that common utensil
Dream up what they do and it's all in the same enterprise.

[224]

So read it and find out that life's a perpetual quest
For what can be decently made, and then be improved.
With stories and pictures he shows you how pencils
    progressed
From a stick in the sand to the mass-produced pencils you've
    loved.

Libraries. A Celebration

The Mitchell, Brynmor Jones and Andersonian,
Delightful Bailey's when it lived in Blythswood Square;
The Reference Room of Paisley Public Library
And Renfrew County's branch beside the cinema –
Of thee I sing and of thy careful catalogues,
Oak tables rubbed with municipal contract polish
By dawn cleaners and anonymous mop-women.
For twenty backroom girls in Marchfield Avenue
At the unfashionble end of the book trade
I offer up these prayers to The Nine Muses
Mentioning that you did not discriminate between
Volumes by half-wits, ninnies and sparkling geniuses,
Tables of Logarithms and *The Divine Comedy*.
The Scottish Association of Assistant Librarians'
Weekend Conference at The Covenanters' Inn –
Dear God, forgive the overdose of venison
And the gluttonous bombast of beer and Beaujolais,
Intensive seminars on 'Libraries Today'.
Luminous digits of the Dewey Decimal System,
UDC and the numbers and letters of Library of Congress,
Compute their shelf-marks on a democratic abacus;
They all go into the stacks, grammatical errors
Eating into posthumous shame like maggots

To say nothing of the acidity of lies
Or worthy thoughts that smoulder on the shadowed shelves.
Tunes and geraniums for Akron Public Library!
Songs, too, for the lady librarians of Ohio
In white-frame rural libraries that looked like farms!
Come back, all ye enthusiasms of yesteryear
Into a retrospective ode's proclaimed rhapsodics...
O the joy of the clunk, opening the Compactus!
And the mischief in puncturing day-dreaming silence,
Dropping the dead-weight of Webster's *Dictionary*
Flat to the floorboards from the height of my chest.
Remember the readers, of more varieties than Heinz
Ever imagined among his alphabets of pasta,
As numerous as beans, as plentiful as soup.
The middle-aged black in Akron at his favourite table
Reading *The Journal of Negro History* end-to-end
Behind a Kilimanjaro of books on Africa
And every book written by blacks in America,
When asked what he was doing, smiled at me, and said,
'Invisible examinations on the subject of skin.
Hey, boy! You, go get me this, if you have it.'
Or the young man in Port Glasgow, studying madly
For raggedy credentials, poverty's homework,
The table-slog of his instinctive scholarship.
Or my old boss, Philip Larkin, holding a book
Written in Indonesian, published in Djakarta,
As if it were a toad that spoke back to him, saying,
'Isn't it *wonderful*? That someone *understands* this?'
Ye glossy students at last-minute mastery
In reading-rooms, posed in multiple solitudes
And making eyes at each other over the tables
In the erotic silences of scholarship!
O ye anonymous reader who marked your place

With a rasher of bacon, will I ever forget you?
O all ye ancient ladies once on waiting-lists
For Pope-Hennessy's *Queen Mary*, and little boys
Imagining armadas in Jane's *Fighting Ships*!
Philosophy and all the -ophies! Fiction! Drama!
Soft toys, soft-core, directories, encyclopaedias!
Romances, westerns,'tec-tales, purchased by the yard!
The arts and sciences, the children's library!
All libraries at night are sleeping giants.
O ye Chief Librarians of Scotland in your good suits!
Celebrities of SCONUL, ASLIB and the *J. of Doc.*,
Associates, Fellows and Office Bearers of the Library
     Association,
Hear this! – the wheels of my retrieval system running
On lubricants of print and permanent devotion!

Bagni di Lucca
Elizabeth Barrett Browning

'Keeping us fresh with shadows...'

October's messengers have come
From up ahead, bearing invisible errands
     On September's winds.
     Visionary autumn
Performs its business as a go-between
Trusted with rumours. Numberless and green
     Upheavals shake the foliage:
There seems no limit to this land of leaves
     As ridge surpasses ridge
On misted Apuan heights where no one lives
Beyond perched settlements, a peopled air

Founded around a sacred bell.
The world is waving. Its *Farewell*
    Shivers in everything
    As green transacts with red,
Kindling the canopy, and wooded hills
    Promise with mottled multiples
A loveliness of leaves before they're shed.
    What can the future bring
Other than what's already lived and dared,
Written, imagined, teeming in your head,
A song to speak, but not a song to sing?
    Always, you're unprepared
For this perception of the Luccan woods
As if eternity's discovered time,
Moving against the body. Solitudes
Seethe in the timbered, many-prayered
    Rolling Apuan sublime.
    Melancholy clocks
Re-measure lifetimes now with louder tocks.
Chestnuts topple on lanes where coaches creak
With clients for the waters, roués, toffs,
Aristocratic, raffish, or antique,
    Some with their towel-wrapped coughs,
Casino fortune-hunters broken down
By dissipated appetites, excess,
    Debauchery, licentiousness,
Turning a village into Europe's town,
Its continental sickness everywhere
And autocratic laughter in the air.
    You catch sight of the truly sick
Who feel as you do for these oceanic
    Murmuring colours in the trees.
You listen as a squeaking local cart

Drowns out the chit-chat of the spa resort
        And leaf-mortalities.
Your boy paddles in the dry drifts, his hand
Held up, and only you can understand
His grasping at a leaf as others fall,
Its terrible, absurd presentiment
    Smeared on your mind, and not at all
The sort of thought with which you feel at home,
    A morbid prophecy, a hint
Depicting lyric sorrow and a leaf
Light in its falling, weightless, perfect, brief
        In its beauty, accurate
In what it makes you feel while watching it.
Aristocrats stroll from their hydrous cures,
Princelings and bankers, withered paramours
From Petersburg, Vienna, London, Rome.
    Wealth on parade, *spirituel* . . .
Imposters, swillbowls, panders, pimps and cranks,
A half-dead dandy drunk by the Lima's banks:
Political and ruthless Christendom
    Flirts with its fashionably ill.
You finger-write these truth-words on the glass –
    TREES HUSBAND POETRY DEATH
    And then erase them with your breath.
        You see a stray leaf pass
    The window where you've rubbed the pane
    Into its unnamed light again.
    Old women in the courtyard know
    What day it is. Each twig-toed broom
Scratches at time on stone-cold pools of shadow.
        There's no elbow-room
Granted by ticking clocks and passing days.
What should we do, other than write, sing, praise

The best in life and us, and being brave
With what we have, and what we do not have?
        Dusk drops Etruscan skies
On Ponte down below, where coats and hats
Stroll by the Lima. Pleasure's plutocrats,
Called by an orchestra to candlelight,
        Shall dine with wasted Dukes tonight
        On Europe of the tears and lies.
        'Oh, husband, lover, nurse,
Last year we climbed by donkey to such heights
It took no effort to caress the stars
And I felt well and strong enough to risk
A lifetime of these elevated nights
Instead of sick-beds, rooms, ink, paper and desk'.
        You look around your room –
A pen, your books, a looking-glass, your comb,
    Gather to you, Elizabeth,
Portable heirlooms and unhappened death.
        Breathe on those glass words once again.
Polish the death-word with your handkerchief.
A spirit waltzes, falling, light as a leaf
        And light and lyric as the song
Sung on the street to cure you of what's wrong
Though what you hear is what the forests cry:
'Time, soon, to leave this house, and start to die'.
        O bella libertà! O bella!

Australian Dream-Essay

They're selling outsize sweaters by the roadside near Coffs
    Harbour.
Deep-fried jacaranda blossom, candied flame-tree petals,
Appeal like hot cakes to heavy-spending Californian tourists
Driving down the length of the Bellinger valley from the
    weird escarpment
Searching its temperate bigness with covetous eyes.

Thousands of black fellers are conjuring up giant kangaroos,
Megapode monsters bursting free from televised fossils
To bounce towards Armidale and such towns looking for
    trouble.
I shut my eyes and magic shows me encyclopaedic pictures.
Thousands of Bar-Bs sizzle into action on nocturnal beaches.
In the morning their charred pocks will look like melanomas.
Surf parades with invisible, haywire percussion, the same roll
Delivered for ever with infinite watery variations.
I can hear the Pacific's micro-ticks between grains of salt.
Dawn's roisterers relax around many beach fires
Listening to one of them pull slow tunes from an accordion.
Each muscled note tells you he practises on a chest-expander.
Disco-whispers waft from the coastal pizza towns.

I walked with some black fellers and visited boulders;
I fitted my hand on secret meanderoids. They did, too;
And the boulders became red hot then burst into flames.
I got lost among megafauna, and when I found myself
Three spinsters gave me tea on their cool veranda.
They'd set sail from Glasgow a hundred and fifty years ago.
Groggy on Old Bush, I mounted my horse and headed for
    Nowhere.
You can get to like certain places in less than a minute.

Songs of lost loggers seeped through time's membrane.
There's much to be said for a country with Nowhere in it,
The least controversial province, peopled by mounted loners
Looking for the wandering legend of themselves and
       forefathers.

A large poet stood up and recited his eucalypt verses.
Only here have I seen men and women in shorts applaud
       poetry.
It isn't ordinary. It's both ordinary and exceptional –
Which is how it should be. His name is Les Murray.
I found myself jumping up and down with approval.
Take a time-tested language and live it on dissimilar
       landcapes
Far from the names and places that gave it its noise
And the shapes of the country that gave it its accents and
       rhythms.
Grow up saying the names of Australia and you won't be
       English,
Irish, Scots, Welsh, Italian, Slav, Greek, Asian or whatever;
You'll just be who you are with a weakening claim on
       grandparents'
European or Asian nostalgia, bad blood and violence.
I like almost everyone, especially Australians.
Some of them, with several conspicuous exceptions, are
       devoted to life, love and liberty.
What get in the way are their origins. What gets in the way is
       us.
Grant them a deserved identity, and they'll teach us
       something.
It will be in a version of our over-used and very tired
       language.

Disenchantments

'It is a world, perhaps; but there's another.' – Edwin Muir

I

Microbiologizing love, despair,
Delight, bountiful dregs, the pulse can stick
On its heirloom heartbeat. The wear-and-tear

Inherited by who-we-are, echoic
Molecular chronology, begins
At birth. Congenital, genetic,

Against know-nothing, careless inclinations,
Death starts with prophecies half-heard in dreams'
Instinctive narratives. A life's toxins –

Psycho-pollution, maverick spiremes –
Gather like gut-data in the underjoyed
Body's puddles, sponges, muscles, pumps and streams.

All sorts of nastiness lead to the void
On wheels of rotten luck or bad habits,
Cirrhosis, hepatitis B, typhoid,

Mournful *-omas*, murder's vast whodunnits;
Or what we do, or what is done to us,
Those little treacheries, the scolds and frets

Being alive receives from generous
Distributors of selfishness. Over
And over, these can really do for us

As much as age. Competitive disfavour
Churns in the psycho-clock's vascular closet,
Timing private sickness, undercover

Birthday chronometers, almost illicit,
They are so personal; and they contain
Everything, seasons, sky, and the explicit

Derivatives of love, delight, fear, pain,
Betrayals, disappointments. Hereafter
Looks like sacred vision; but it's profane –

God's salesmanship, then His religious laughter.

II

The dead can't talk, or appear on your doorstep,
Or be discovered turning to you from
Beautiful landscapes, wearing smiles of courtship,

Perusals of what you've written about them.
Only in life's interior extra sense
Are they glimpsed, tending a geranium

While gathered strangely into a presence
Reality shudders at, holding off
Memory's insults to the intelligence.

Walking out of the light, a breeze's puff
By a window, you might think, where blue
Silvers on glass; and that could be enough

By itself, but someone's looking at you,
Real and unreal, inside you and outside,
A figment of the dead, the past, but true,

No matter dithering agnostic pride
Saying, 'What-is most certainly *is-not*,
But, if you must, it *might* be clarified

'By that misplaced and found-again snapshot,
That placemark concert-ticket, old days
Remembered by a pleasure that you bought

'Together in another time, always
Enslaved by the sudden, and overthrown
By unbecoming rediscoveries.'

I can make contact through the gramophone
Via Duke Ellington. So, am I mad?
Or, as the man says, am I merely prone

To accidental confabs with the dead
On the ghost-line, splicing the mainbrace
With brimful goblets of Burgundy red

While breathy missives wing through inner space?
'Don't bug me, friend. I've got a rendezvous
To keep with the transfigured commonplace.'

'It's then we think we see God. Which isn't true.
Or when you see your past objectified.'
'If anything, it's when God looks at you,

'Or who-you-were is walking by your side,
Half-meaningful, half-meaningless, but clear,
Past-self and present matching stride for stride.'

A window dribbles with a double tear.

III

Hereafter? No, the here and now, wonders
Far from a window's figurative thaws.
How mind moves leads the spirit into blunders

Against the grain of life and all its laws.
Hereafter? Yes, but it's in memory.
Lifetimes like loose and lacy gauze

Float through their weightless doors and fly away
When light lies like a creature on the floor
And life hereafter seems an ordinary

Conclusion to be drawn. It's not décor
For healed broken-hearts, nor occult stasis
Cultured by fairy-tale enchanted lore

From self-inflicted schizo-Christian praxis —
It happens in the eye and intellect.
Life tells you that it doesn't, but it does.

And so we say it's something we suspect
Can happen, but when it does, we turn away,
Convinced experience is incorrect

Or that the weather's curdled Saturday
Into phenomena of foliage,
Water, sky, explicable, but too risky

To ask your mind to cross an unsafe bridge
Between its preconceptions and the sense
Cradled in other realms in wordless language,

Preferring a quotidian self-defence
Against time's birdsung waggishness and tricks
Eavesdropping on a dialect with no tense.

Ignoring, too, who caused those sudden physics.
Neglecting, also, feeling, and a brief
Inveiglement from life beyond its ethics.

Turning your back on yourself. Shunning grief.

Sky and the Firth become five flying swans.
It might as well be the twelfth century –
There's nothing on the eye other than bygones,

Nothing 'modern' (whatever that might be)
To wreck a day's half-finished wilderness
Or undermine a moment's witchery.

My eyes wear glass. Twentieth-century dress
All over me, but medieval thinking
For several minutes as I retrogress

Into preposterous ancestry's winking
Annals and declarations. Pine-cones, thorns,
Cathedral silence and monastic drinking,

Pre-Reformation winds, primeval ferns,
Scrub-scratchy woodlands and druidic oaks,
Show antique Scotland. Static me unlearns

Feral history, and shuns its tribal jokes,
Learning instead – truly, it feels like loss –
Identity, while distant stubble smokes

Against eternal blue. Lyrical dross,
Four shades of it, smoke-purpled blue, sky-blue,
Firth's water-turquoise, is the blue chaos

Mind makes of it. Intelligence, askew,
Sunk in anachronism's precious keek
Into an everlasting Firth-wide view,

Hears timeless anger in a cart-wheel's squeak
On an old drover's road – another time,
Of the beginning emigrants, the shriek

Deep in the nineteenth century's sublime
Diaspora, when Scottish refugees
Bucked landlords, penury and sheepish crime.

Ontario and the Antipodes,
Montana, Texas, and an upside-down
Deracinated patriotism overseas,

Emerge from aerogrammes in a ghost town
Sealed by the spit of families who headed
Into salt, cast-offs of the British Crown.

Therefore that roofless ruin, rot-shredded
Rafters sprinkled among ferns and bleak briars,
Air an infertile pause where much childbedded

Women fed turf into the constant fires,
Kept up the names, filled buckets at the well,
Reared sons for work, or none, and an empire's

Nomadic armies. Graveyard of the snail-shell
And captive household botany, home to
Forgotten people, a timid harebell

Growing in shadow, now it's become pure blue
Roof, door and windows, home of open air,
Gravestone, unwritten names, memorial dew.

I had my moments in the disrepair
Time rippled into on a Firth-side hill,
Visions of then's dilapidated prayer.

Depopulated place, its physical
Selfhood was beautiful; its country shone –
Sky, water, ruins, five swans, and the still

Untimed lucidity my mind moved on.

V

What's real is suffering's not the mystique
Tragedies pump it up with. Selfish truth –
Too difficult to write, too sore to speak –

Abandons pain to poetry's lyric sleuth –
Deerstalker, pipe, and magnifying glass –
Or mid-life critic in the undergrowth

Sniffing the rhythmic stench of language-gas
While hunting down the poet on the beach
Or where he/she lurks by the underpass.

Sorrow, delight, and mysteries of speech
Turned on a sentient metre, flatter us.
What has a decent poetry left to teach?

It can repeat, describe, bespatter us
With not-being-Shakespeare-Milton-Byron-Keats...
Don't ask for flight. New poets are apterous.

Post-this, post-that – pre-*what*? The obsolete's
Established as a form (like this), parodic
Purloining of a thirteenth-century beat,

Dante's drum-kit, a metronomic tick,
While those intent on being 'of the Age'
Doodle devoutly in a Bolshevik

Modernist manner's nervous prose, a rage
Easy to sympathize with, but harder to
Believe (impossible, in fact), no gauge

For being alive in 1992
When life seems threatened by the very nasty
And an Apocalypse chirps *Peekaboo*

Through fissures in the sky, that very vasty
Surrounding substance of the sun and stars.
Toast Hell in Scotch, then gargle well with Asti!

Incinerated loves and burnt memoirs
May well remember quaffs like these
On speechless evenings of the grievous jars

When sorrow's nib sipped comfort from the lees
But thought it dipped in the Pierian Sink
Instead of grief's deep cistern of litotes.

Sorrow comes out, and then goes down to drink
As shy gazelles do in the wildlife films,
Poking their noses in capricious ink.

Creatures are perfect. They don't need pseudonyms.
They can't tell lies. All their events are true.
Full force of memory, before it dims –

The weight of wisdom dwindles into dew.

VI

Back to the point, although I doubt if point
Can be the term, and so I think will you
Consider after-life delusion's vaunt.

Some have their landscapes for that big to-do
Few folk believe in, or hope for when they're dead.
'When I die, I would like to go to...'

How often have bedside-sitters heard *that* said
In voices dying simplifies with truth?
I think my father's was his garden shed.

They speak from innocence, in tones of youth
From a white and retrogressive deathbed-land
Where nothing's worried, guilty or uncouth.

Mine might be a certain starlit headland –
I feel silly saying it, but there it is,
My very own unnecessary zed-land.

The dream you die into, whatever it is,
Infinite leisure, or a religious
Promise well kept, or brilliant, effortless

Sex, tennis and Montrachet can comfort us
Immensely, the eternal winning try
At Murrayfield, a long kick's fictitious

Glory made literal for ever. Why,
Anyone could get to like a Paradise
Devoted to the ego's pastimes. We'd die

To get to where imagination's lies
Come true, where who you are is who you want
To be or what you'd like to fantasize

In a perpetual hour-glass that you'll haunt
Siftingly, until you're very bored, dogged
By people like Dante and Billy Beaumont,

Big blokes who'll knock you down, or have you flogged
For not being up to scratch, Pastor Jack Glass
And Christians who *will* have you catalogued

In one or other less-than-paradisal class
Fit only for the kitchen's out-of-bounds
Or scissoring a lawn's celestial grass

While they and people like them ride to hounds.
No, make mine pagan, please, Republican,
Domestic, set in very private grounds,

A spacious grave where all five senses quicken.

VII

Oblivion, eternal zilch, demands
Heroic pluck, if that's what you have faith in.
Those personal, very private Never-Lands

Construct nirvana. Don't think – imagine!
It won't be good for you; and there are days
When I believe in grey rivers and boatmen

In shabby cloaks. I got stuck in a maze
Once in a Wonder Book. My pencilled line
Just couldn't get me through fifty wrong ways

To reach the treasure. Talk about serpentine...
False trails led crookedly to Minotaurs.
Whoever drew it was a loathesome swine

For whom a puzzle meant locking all doors,
Switching lights off, worse than Madame Tussaud's
Nasties in her Chamber of Horrors.

We'd all refuse a blindfold at our gallows,
Stakes, guillotines, or kneeling at the grave
Dug by ourselves, spading a life's shallows

After the paths we chose to walk, and pave
With good intentions, proved deplorable.
So, carry on, pretending to be brave;

A tear or two is quite forgivable.
Get that over, and then get over it;
But don't forget your guilty, culpable

Ethical errors – remorse is infinite.
Wrong perhapses, wrong noes and wrong yesses
Don't half increase a moral deficit –

Pissy, isn't, it, when sin's caresses
Smother you with sick kisses? It's shitty.
Involuntarily, life evanesces

Into famous last words, the nitty-gritty –
'Bugger Bognor!' 'I want a Forfar bridie!'
And other specimens of witty pity –

'Ach, only one man ever understood me,
And he didn't either.' 'A *double* Scotch,
For God's sake! Where's my fags and ashtray?'

A de-pulsed wrist with its still-ticking wrist-watch
Presents how life goes clocking ever onward
While someone's laughing on the street, your crotch

Itching as if with disrespect, swear-word
Of your own body, sacramental curse
Crossed with the secular, and both absurd –

An undertaker farting in his hearse.
Come, cancer, coronary, firing-squad;
But seldom in these several lines of verse

Speak ill of Him, monosyllabic God.

'You thought you'd died? You thought you'd really died?'
Says a cheeky biographer who knows
More than he should of vanity and pride.

His subject's lyric loves turn into prose.
Diaries! Photocopied indiscretions!
Nightmare, scholarly scenarios!

All that privacy, the famous reticence,
Printed! Transmitted secrets! Microphoned
Betrayals, squalor, sloth, lust, dalliance,

Become posterity's testosteroned
Chapters in which the reader gasps and laughs.
Footnoted bottles – *oo-ya*! – and he's a boned

Kippered cadaver whose recorded gaffes
Might leave you thinking you're as bad as he was –
Blared, blurted, broadcast inner paragraphs!–

And offer up a late, heartfelt applause.
What's much more likely is you'll think you're better
Or victim of a justifiable cause

Of bad behaviour, being a go-getter,
While X was passive, Y a dolt, and Z
Pathetic. There was nothing could unfetter

That proud, demented sod. Now that he's dead
Judgemental majesty sits in its court
And gives the prurient the go-ahead.

Posterity? It's literary sport.
It's sordid literature, counting maggots
Before it rubber-stamps, or not, a passport

To the critical glades, kingdom of wits
Perfect in life and work. Oh, dearie me! –
Poetry's after-life, controlled by shits.

Parnassus! Helicon! Don't weary me
With 'reputation', 'text', 'context', or 'fame';
Don't '-ize' or '-ism' me; don't 'theory' me –

The consequence of poetry is shame.

IX

Sundry tawdry wee filths, etcetera,
Mendacity, adultery, and drink's
Magical transport to its Riviera

(Though you're transformed into an androsphinx)
Could see you written down by chatterboxes;
And *there*'s your after-life – high jinks, *low* jinks,

Your gluttonies portrayed as paradoxes
Frogmarched across pages. Shame is the spur!
What's left of you gets filed in little boxes.

You're in a big one, though. A character,
Fictitious now, you're up for grabs.
God help you if there's nothing there to slur,

Byronic naughties, pox, or other scabs
For posthumous picking, Burnsian pranks,
Elopements, opium, and nocturnal cabs

To roister-houses where the lady spanks –
You're guaranteed remembrance if you're bad!
Biography loves roués, twerps and cranks.

Who'd read about a saint, when there's a cad
To entertain the literary punter's
Ethical tastes in tales of Jack-the-Lad?

Wordsworthian paternity chunters
In fat books. I feel sorry for Wordy,
Hunted down, and nailed, by the truth's head-hunters.

Boring Wordsworth, his morals weren't sturdy,
Or so the story seems to say, performed
On howling truth's censorious hurdy-gurdy.

Denunciation's dirty ear feels warmed
By damnatory music's dissonance
Through which the mind's informed, or misinformed,

It hardly matters which. Truth prints its licence
Much as lies do. Biography's imagined.
Subjects can look conspicuous by their absence.

If there's an after-life, it's in the mind
Of anyone who thinks about the dead
With what respect or disrespect's examined

By knowledge. There are people in my head
Whom I shall never see again or talk to
Although I dream of what they *might* have said

When I appeal to what they'd have me do
In a crisis, when making a choice
Means I might need advice to see me through

A pickle they would understand – *that* voice
No longer in the world, though I can make it
Happen so very easily, so close

It's closer than in the room. I fake it;
That's after-life, and though there might be more,
I wouldn't want to try to William Blake-it.

I have my ghosts to see. Intimate lore
Rides out from curtains over puddled light
And feels expected when a draughted door

Opens on emptiness. Unvoiced *Goodnight*
Propels its micro-whisper's spectral bye-bye
Into my head, and gives me quite a fright.

Worst soundtrack possible – seeing your life's sigh
Mirrored, re-echoed indistinct remorse,
A big noise on the spirit's glassy hi-fi –

But once you've heard it sobbing itself hoarse
In your own throat, and then let that hundredth
Nightmare exhaust its visionary force

In your nervous system, its dismal myth
Informing part of you, *that's* when you own
Your miserable life entirely. Sackcloth.

Mineral loneliness. The hour of stone.
A boat cut loose. Not much to steer it with.
Grey branches hanging over Acheron.

Look to the living, love them, and hold on.

Moorlander

His name began in legend at
No fixed address, next door
To hawthorns and a twisted birch.
His ancestry's recorded in
Absent chronicles, the unresolved
Transactions of his name and place,
And not in Edinburgh, nor
In any parish register
On or off the Scottish map.
Parentage and where he came from
Are as mysterious to us
As a whaup's dreams, witherty-weeps'
Pluvial metaphysics.

His body aches with footsore wilderness,
Burghs, streets, firths, seasonal miles
To cities seen at night from high places.
Strath, carse, mains, bal, mearns, dun, pit, auchter,
For, easter, wester, kil, drum, inver, aber, inch –
He runs like silent ballad, rumour, or
Black water, plotting courses by
Star-fix, fragrant month, and distant farms
Whose lights chink from a curtain or a door.
He is map and shadow – *brae*, *law*, and *ben* –
That fast corner of darkness
That was on the edge of the headlamps.

Scholarly trackers stir
Embers, maukins' bones,
Plucked feathers from a stolen hen.
They miss him by days and weeks.
He is downwind of their civilization.

They stalk him with tape recorders,
Cameras and disappointment's notebook.
In three languages, he impersonates
Water, gersie brae, swan, laverock,
Sionnach, curlew, and dòbhran.
He can go as an earth-trout.
He is as hoof, paw, and stealthy wing.
He can turn into tree or rock;
In winter he sleeps as such
Camped on misfortune's moorland.
Bog-cotton, tormentil, and the upland rose,
These, too, are in his repertoire,
His transformations, his metamorphoses.
Tread carefully; you don't know who they are.

Nomad, pity's statistic,
He journeyed into back-time, a ditch-lord's
Anachronism. Time turned into place.
Society gave up its ghost,
Geography its nationhood;
He put on hodden grey and climbed
Into resistant solitude.
He is the man without windows and doors.
His furniture is horizontal,
Stone, turf, or fallen timber,
Or it is the ground's hammock.
His windows are yours and mine.
Also his doors.

Infinity's emigrant,
The man who was here first
Before the road west awa' yonder
Opened America, he stirs
Mythical brose

In his fern-roofed pantry
Above an oat-coloured firth
And its high shroud of conifers.
Dusk falls with a relish for rest and beauty,
As always, as something eternal
That knows no defeat or controversy,
As sunrise, a taken-for-granted
Sameness of self with the weather.
His is the sole, licensed fire
On the hillside, a flickering smeddum,
A relic of what once was merry.
West awa' yonder, south awa' yonder...
Spirit at home now, indignant,
Exhausted, our new-minted ferlie –
   'Tis this I hope and dreid,
   *Man is enchantit to the deid'.**

    * Lewis Spence, 'The Ferlie'

The Crossroads of the Birds

High on the draining ridges, a road is blue
Reflected puddles for a laverock's
Mirrored lyric; and he is here, the true
Beggar, ancestral and unorthodox.

It is the time of the crucifix, old
Pre-Reformation days and a bad year
For war; the hairst is sour and thin, and its cold
Tenantry deaf to stonechat and wheatear.

Men with steel hands are riding on this road.
He hears them miles away, then sniffs the rain
Approaching through a lowered warmth as cloud
Covers the sun, and it begins again –

A supplicant, his head hooded, his hand
Held out towards the narrow thunder's roar,
The other on his staff. Summer moorland
Tilts into scented space and a downpour

Where three roads meet. Braked hoofs and fisted reins
Fill the snort-broken silence, trampled mud,
Tapped breastplates, an equestrian fragrance
He speaks into from mortal solitude...

He feels his hood pushed back as a cold sword
Prods through his hair, so that the man they see
Where three roads meet above a gurgling ford
Stands eyeless in his whiskered beggary,

The stretched skin stitched, religious needlework
Performed by Black Friars in the Canongate.
After the screaming blaze, a painful, dark
Survival. Hunger, footsteps, miles, narrate

Disfigured life that cannot see itself,
Alert in other senses. 'Wairdwood! Which way,
Blind man?' Fierce joke. A thrown penny's pelf,
A muddy coin, a mutilated day.

'Over the ford, lords, to the forge of Wairdwood,'
He answers, pointing. 'It's two saddle-hours
North to the anvils, and my word is good.
I promise you the road across these moors.

'God's arle, kind sirs? For charity and God!'
Laughter, then leather, horse and soldiery
Ride on with fifty noises to their road,
The startled heron at the stream, this story

Already chronicled and sung, its notes
Spreading by finch-song, passing through the air
On balladry, through narrative throats,
And told in Wairdwood long before they're there,

Told in another tongue than this, spoken by
Starlight, bog-cotton speech, told, and re-told
At the dragonflies' graveyard. Passers-by
Listen to language, sung, unbegged, unsold.

'Bare Ruined Choirs'
'To a blind student that hath the Irish [i.e. Gaelic] language, 3d.'
Cramond, *Church of Rathven*

Bird-song and running water, sounds such as
    Weather makes, one thing on
Another, rain, leaves, thatch, the wind and grass
    Breathing ... When audible Anon
Sings to a blind man, any parish feels
    As nature's nation or
His own. An unseen miller's unseen wheels
    Quoted their stone, agrarian murmur.

What happens ends up written down. It speaks
    Inaccurate events,
False anecdotes, hints, covert verbal keeks
    Into unwritten testaments.

A nationless and local thrush sang there
    Beyond all history.
Unlettered life inscribed itself on air,
    Its song-life in a vocal tree.

Miles from your languge that I'm blood and years
    Remote from, you would sense
Translated pity when the kirk's cashiers
    Assessed your sightlessness in pence
And Lallan speech, its spittle, lilt and lift,
    Already looking south
With ear and pen prepared to catch the drift
    Accented in an English mouth.

Unhappened Homer, dream-Bard, Ossianic
    Figment, Gaelic silence
Settles between each scratching of your stick
    On the bare road, stopping to rinse
Your mouth out with a line of song, disgrace
    On your extended hand,
Your three warm poor-box coins, kirk, trade, and place,
    One for each language of this land.

Big-weathered landscapes measure their laments
    In triple tongues, a plack
For each maimed witness and its discontents;
    And I am walking at your back,
Whatever your life, where, when, or what you did
    Off-history or in
Dimensionless parishes, the unrecorded
    Best left to an imagination

At a warm stretch. Your stick shall guide me there
    With a penny in my purse
By your unchosen heathered thoroughfare.
    Indigenous prosodic morse
Beats out the landmarks in its rhythmic braille
    And, with your eyes, I climb
Resentment's mountain, where a stick-touched trail
    Ends in a country west of time.

The Penny Gibbet

Wearing a badge to prove his pauperdom's
Licensed, official, therefore no disgrace
To the parish and the marching kettledrums,
But grounded deep in lawfulness and place,

He chooses where to stand, a blue-gowned man
Between the barrowed cripples and the tall
Two orphaned daughters of the cateran
They hanged a year ago. Good copper dole

That day by the gallows, as soon as death
Startled the crowds and prophesied their own –
Post-mortem charity when strangled breath
Froze in the air, a daughter's Gaelic moan

Chilling the deed. Now there are other throats
Brought here to weight the frosted ropes today.
A loyal beggar, hungering for groats
In the morning, by the guarded carpentry –

'*God Save the King*!' – transacts his livelihood.
A garrison of Union marches up
On its dynastic tread, and gratitude,
Servility and hate, chink in the cup.

Gaberlunzie

He sinks in. He lives in my mind's attic
Far gone in journeys as the clock turns back
On its centuries, each disnumbered tick
A loosening of time's events. The slack
Clockwork regresses on its moments as
His vagrancy sightsees the way it was
With gathered sorners in forgotten eras
Borrowing board by force and bread with blows.
Seventeenth-century footprints tracked in frost
Ascend in morning, skirting the hedgerows
Before the sun's touch melts the grassy crust
And ploughland browns through its de-silvered furrows.
So, as he walks this field, the man I see
Wears distant rags, stooping on his own strut
By the sloped edge of woods, for his secrecy
Demands a deep escape into the shut
Glades and gullies, wild country where he's safe
Among bracken, in his hideouts of fern –
Gaberlunzie, half-life, national waif,
Earth-pirate of the thistle and the thorn.

Nineteen-Thirteen

A couple in a single-end, one room,
One window with its curtain drawn,
Torn, dirty, and keeping out
Nothing of the rolling stock's
Incessant full employment.
Steam, noise and smoke
Disguise the blackened stone
On which the many tracks are raised.
They're bathing a dead baby in an enamel basin –
Gently, water from her cupped hand
Dipping and rinsing as she croons
Maternal lullabies.
She's bitter that her man
Should weep like this, sobbing
And spoiling what she must preserve.

Weeding a Border

Forget our scientists, inventors, and others
Working with mathematics and materials
Or minds chasing abstractions and infinity –
We are a people of expeditionary botanists.
Geology defines our minds and verse?
Rubbish! 'Stone for a stony heart' says all.
Devoutly may that infatuation be avoided.
Instead, think of our love of the leaf,
Our fathers, into whom we grow, tending
Chrysanthemums and dahlias at sunset
Beside a wheelbarrow and a watering-can.
Perfect carrots, the cold-frame, beetroot, lettuce,

Potatoes, and glamorous Byzantine gladioli,
These, too, are native, and express the way
A country's drawn to pleasure, as do also
Delicate sweetpeas, succulent runner-beans.
– *Respublica; république; la chose publique*:
Difficult issues steeped in mellow life's
Agreeable distractions, our words causing
Stammering embarrassment, unable to prise free
Beauty, bird-song, preferable politics.

Body Echoes

The man who disappeared in skylined scrub
Where stone was cut for minor bridges, byres,
Farmhouses, orchard walls (requarried for
Suburban patios or sunk to hold
Whooshed, Hadrianic banks of Motorways)
Turns out to be the same man as the one
Who waited at the milestone by the plinth
With milkchurns, where the country backroads bus
Drew up at his unnecessary wave
Back in the Fifties. Then, the man was old.
The man I saw up on the chiselled ridge
Levered his lean, athletic silhouette
Against the doors of April, entering
Yesterday's settlements, fields, streets and rooms
No longer on the parish map, erased,
Still showing, though, stone and grass residue
Detectable to eyes familiar with
The Voters' Roll of 1956.
Each is the same man as the young man seen
On Monday at a harbour in the east

Defying time and compass, where his brief
Marine appearance vanished into morning –
Sun on the Tay, an atmospheric stir,
An increase in the April temperature
As off he went on movements of the water,
On watery wheels, on blue light-stoked machines.
    And the woman I've seen, his age always,
From young to old, she walks in other districts.
North, south, east and west, fields and villages,
Cities and mountains, shed the present tense
To reconstruct a monstrous permanence.
In shops I go to, she's been seen waiting
At electronic tills that become counters
In former Co-ops in the former burghs –
Dingwall in 1926, Sanquhar
In a postponed, old, modern year, Dumfries
On any date after the ruined peace
Described as pre- or post-War, those events
Recalled by old men, celluloid and print
In towns where war memorials list more names
Than 1918's Telephone Directory
For anywhere named for biscuits or bridies
Or towns in Canada, South Africa,
Australia, New Zealand and the USA.
Used time is answerless, continuing
Its waste of life, so who and when they were
Repeat themselves, over and over again.
Light, land and water, the triple acclaim
Beauty enjoys when birded lilacs shake
With vocal loveliness and light is sung,
Try to disprove such sorrow, but they can't.
I've seen him walk at night in several places
Within our borders, and the national moon

Devoured him as he strode beyond his years
In the thistle gardens by the railway,
Someone for whom the future's worse than wrong.
He is as footsteps – *Is he? Isn't he?* –
Headed through etymologies and names,
Industrial herbage, frontier overgrowth,
Tangles of wild thorn, wilderness timber,
Into an unrecorded country that
Historians don't know of. If they do
They fear its absence of modernity,
Its unresolved remorse, its carelessness
With land and water, measuring the light
But not its beauty, nor its spirit, nor
How past and present are unreconciled
As any broken love, like theirs, and this
Hurts reason, as he does, and as she does –
Is she? Isn't she? – She is; and he is, too.
I've seen her stand outside a factory's gates
As if the gates and factory were there,
Expecting him among a booted shift –
That smell of foundries like a metal wind
Wafted from molten rose-beds, sharpened on
Industry, rent, ore, marriages and children.
Those tenements, the way they tumbled down
In the slow motion of history! –
Into the dumper trucks, as fodder for
Modernity's big fill-ins, Glasgow's stone
In buried middens where its bogles howl.
    Against the sounds of the sea, a roof-top dove
Performs its throated wooing. Much bird-song,
Chirping courtships, this twenty-fourth of March
By a window where a St Andrews garden
Shows off a bright azalea and a palm

In a Himalayan boast crossed with hot
Tropical green, a girl shaking her hands
At a sink. It has very deep sweetness,
This moment, colossal sugar, brilliant
Ambrosial light, and I almost forget
The woman I saw earlier today
From Innes's corner, crossing South Street,
When time wrinkled and the cars changed, years
Unwound themselves in a reversed photoflood.
I had no name to call. I saw a sound
And neither eye nor ear could hold it.
   Time took offence at what they didn't do
Or say or what they did or said, or else
Echoed existence wouldn't be like this
Recurrent riddle that my eyes witness
Out on the rim of who, when, where and why.
I've seen her in a muddy yard, headscarfed,
Soaked, by the door of a spectral byre, or
Heaving her weight against a frosted pump
Or beating passive cattle with a stick.
Is it in love that nationhood begins
To come out right and find the natural
In being and becoming, in politics
That take into account the land and light
And no one in the country goes unheard?
What foolish question's this, to test a mind
Perplexed by beauty and inertia?
They had no country, have not; until then
A nationality of night and day
Identifies them – intimate seasons, years,
Their duplicated journey, searching for
Each other in the mottled parishes
Where children play at hide-and-seek among

Tilted epitaphs and memorial texts
In the necropolis of skull kisses.
I think his death usurped its discipline,
As hers has done, places and years ago,
Two people who have lost their graves and names
Because of who and where they were and are.
Perpetual stories rattle like dried peas
In an old Ostermilk tin, saying the same
Perplexing fiction – 'Happiness is hard.
The ship for Canada leaves in the morning'.
They don't, and didn't, give enough to life,
Meaning each other, everyone, the big
Outline of possibilities, opting
For tears and overrated suffering.
  I've seen her on the street with sorrow's suitcase
With which I've seen her walk, sore with its weight,
Through present commerce on the Nethergate;
And seen him, too, and seen them look alike
At stations, bus depots, in public parks,
Brechin, Renfrew, Dalmellington and Keith,
A man, a woman, separated, but for whom
Patience is part of who and where they are,
Infinite longing but for mortal peace,
National halves, the woman and the man.
Reach with your hands into the dark and hold
And the rivers will flow, filled with many fish,
Sun and clean rain, and the hairst shall be good –
Perth, Selkirk, Inverness, Dunfermline –
Shadows on everywhere and Princes Street.

Poor People's Cafés

Not down-and outs,
Though some come close,
Nor layabouts
Trading pathos
For tea and bread,
But simply poor
In this lowered
Epoch, its door
Stiff to their shoves,
No easy entrance
To decent groves
Of furtherance.

Steamed spectacles
As I sit down
At the wiped spills,
Raising the tone
(Or so it seems)
Against their will.
National dreams
Have gone downhill
And there's a hoax
In every mouth,
Demented jokes
And diddled truth.

Such rooms translate
Half-lies in how
Waitresses wait
On out-at-elbow
Customers by
Puddled sills, drips

From windows. Pie,
Baked beans and chips;
Tea, sausage roll...
That smell of coat;
Dried rain, and a scowl
From a dead thought.

Two women brood;
Their roll-ups burn –
Smoked solitude,
Both taciturn,
Each parodies
In somewhere else;
And somebody's
Companion smells
His burgered plate
Then starts to eat.
Waitresses wait
On slippered feet.

He talks to a cup;
She stirs their tea
Then holds it up,
A wedded pity
In how they share –
Her sip, his sip;
It looks like prayer,
Companionship
In a belief
In the unknown,
Elderly grief
And most hopes gone.

Down in the dumps
Indignant notes
Compile a glimpse
Of huddled coats
And this kitchen's
Primitive broth
Where tendered pence
This twentieth
Day of the dead
Winter, transact
Important bread
And stale neglect.

On these borders
Being poor
Inches towards
Life less than meagre.
Going down, no rest
For the unendowed
And dispossessed.
A public shroud
Conceals their fall
And the public purse
Cuts wherewithal
To make it worse.

'*Mister! Mister!*
Fifty pence, please!
Come oan, come oan, sir!'
Our coins appease
Sore charity,
Expense of shame
And low pity.
And in whose name

But Government's
In Central Station,
Where life's laments
Offend a nation?

Low benefits
Or none at all
And that cap fits
On one and all
Who voted for
'Initiative'
That metaphor
By which they live.
The Devil's in 't,
The way they quest
For self-reliant
Self-interest.

Worse than worse is
How they flatter
'Market Forces' –
Mad as a hatter!
While they grow strong
Others diminish,
From wrong to wrong
Until the finish.
Twenty per cent?
Go, tax their breath!
Jack up the rent!
'Reform', or death!

Ideologue
And Moneybags
Loathe Underdog

And the Man in Rags,
And I imagine
A similar bitch
Calls profits in
To make her rich
From this cheap kitchen,
Where a bad smell slurs
A tawdry nation
And its treasurers.

'Financial link'?
That's what you say?
That's how *you* think?
Put it this way –
I say you stink;
You tax the poor.
'Financial link'?
What is it for?
I'll tell you. Sirs,
And Madams, you
Pretend to answers
As if you knew

The questions, but
You don't. You feel
A need to 'cut'
But not to heal.
'Financial link'?
What is it *for*?
It's how you *think*.
That's what it's for.
Six million souls
In pauperdom;

A round of doles
Till Kingdom-come! . . .

For a' that, aye,
For a' that, men
Could live and die,
The angry pen
Fall from the hand
And nothing change
In this hurt land
Until that strange
Obsession dies
And begging-bowl
Free enterprise
Goes to the wall.

Women who sit
Without a bean
Articulate
The unforeseen –
From opulence
By luck or tick
To indigence
In the bus-district,
The same scrap-heap
As shuttered shops,
That burst downpipe,
Those plundered skips.

'Leave them to root
In the litter-bin;
The destitute
Are guilty of sin.'
Death's dialect

Announces his
Sneered disrespect
And prejudice.
Grim children wait
While mother pays
And it grows late
For the decencies.

Queen February

She is no angel-wind, this
Orphan of orphans, kicked out
Thousands of years ago
From her mother's tragedies.

Poverty is all she's known,
Opulent squalor, rain-rags.
She has no complexion;
She is a child without skin

Fathered by distance on ocean.
Ancient ice, incarcerated water,
Squeaks on millennial centimetres
At the split, glacial cliffs.

She is northhood's daughter,
Victim first, now terrorist,
With her thin howls, emaciated
Chilled visions, refrigerated wrath

Broadcast on her spectacular
Bellows, her Golgothic breath.
Her special gift is to invade
Whole islands and to sweep them

To treeless hygiene, polished rock.
The government of shrubs and trees
Treats for mercy, but branches snap
Where her grey fingers throttle

And go flying as twigs become
Breakages, timber amputees
In the wintry leaflessness
Where light is a month's essence.

Distant trees on a ridge lean
In their submissive silhouettes –
Pale and sinister February,
A crippled slave-grove atop

Thrashed copses, frantic woods,
Shivering coniferous tips.
Her cries are thrawn and vindictive;
She is a hemisphere's affliction,

Its malevolent waif.
I stare into her stormy eye
And her screams crest as I call
To her – '*I am not your enemy.*'

But she is witches' laughter.
There is no talking to her; she is
Colossal unforgiveness,
Mockery, anger, hysteria,

And a man on a ridge feels raped
By this Fury, this Amazon
Giantess with icy lips,
Innumerable flaxen-haired

Lady Viking faces, her shrieks
Exploding from female Valhalla
And lifetimes and lifetimes of wrongs,
From the Siberian Islands.

I'm her momentary plunder,
A psyche to be ransacked, buffeted
By weather that begins in ice.
Her booty's like that – lives,

The men and women she enlists
Or steals. Their bones stuff her caverns.
Their spirits fly with her.
She means to cause trouble, and does.

When I get home, she's there.
She comes in by windows and doors,
Through the plugged chinks in them,
This Lucifer-girl, this rebel

From the world's sculleries and brooms,
Its pantries, dust-pans and sinks,
Its deplorable circumstances,
Hostels, hovels and addictions.

She has no bed or birthday where she sleeps
Among her countless replicas,
Her acolytes, the frozen genders;
She is surrounded by herself

In her stronghold, by cold fire-flesh,
Entwined and sobbing in her streeted caves
As a blizzard whitens darkness
And glaciers pretend to shift.

Audenesques for 1960

Neither very brave, nor very beautiful,
Nor heterosexually inclined, but still, you were
My imaginary mentor, fantasy's ear
Attentive as I twaddled half-baked poetical opinions
Walking to work in Renfrew County Library.

Your voice was culled from two radio broadcasts
Informing the cadences of emulative reading
As of someone learning a difficult new language
In a country where it is rarely heard spoken,
Where, in any case, speech defects are pandemic.

You had become one of your doting readers
Before death claimed you in shadowy Vienna.
You, too, were a way of happening, tongue, teeth, larynx,
Sounding and looking like a demotic Sphinx
Devoted to an eccentric sagacity.

These make-believe walking pow-wows about verse
Permitted you to change my mind, throwing a tantrum,
Saying 'You bloody fool!', with the sinister antics
Of an aggressive and very dangerous parson.
You helped to populate my private madness.

With no one else to speak to on such subjects,
Small wonder, then, that I just made you up.
For thirty minutes of each morning we were both
Fictitious chatterboxes (except that you weren't).
You can learn almost anything if you have to.

'Listening to someone else recite one's verses,
While flattering, is also deeply painful.
Be a good boy, and don't, when I'm about,
Murder "The Fall of Rome" with your Scottish accent's
Rhotacistic R and slobbering lambdacism.'

You never knew about these pedestrian talk-ins.
How could such an embarrassing admission be spoken?
I saw you once only, on the other side of a room.
Self-confident timidity got the better of me.
Admiration is better off left on its own terms.

Strange, though, that seeing you was less thrilling
Than I'd imagined it would have been. After all,
In my repeated, highly informative fictions,
Something as good as trust had been contrived
But for my benefit only, my consolation,

Putting words in your mouth, and holding off
Intellectual loneliness. What effrontery,
Cheek, bumptiousness, and covertly malapert
Transgression on the privacy of a complete stranger!
But I can think of far worse fantasies.

For in those days it seemed that the only metre
Open to me for reading and close inspection
Was one whose ticks measured consumption of gas.
Imagination is Everyman's intimate theatre,
Biological cinema whose programmes run endlessly

Whether as willed dreams, sexual forecasting,
Or memories of what hasn't happened and never will.
Not much is discovered without its rehearsals
Welling up out of inadequacy and aspiration;
But it wasn't nice to have invented someone real.

It was our secret. I forgot to let you in on it.
Sorry. You were more than my useful friend.
Too often, the heartfelt is belated and shameful.
In this case some sort of national distrust –
Not mine, but others' – postponed it for years.

I was angered once by Glaswegians dismissing you as
'The Grand Panjandrum of the Homintern'.
Poetry has too many enemies to contend with.
'A nancy poet, not a real one; and a fake socialist'.
One genius tends to use another as a doormat.

Nationality doesn't identify 'our side'.
Muses are international, and mine is a Lady
Who speaks all sorts of languages (in translation),
Collects guidebooks, maps, timetables, menus,
Wine lists, and other hedonistic souvenirs.

So what if you were English? I speak that language,
But not its nationality; I love your poetry,
And our imaginary talks – I mean, remembering them –
Please me as proof of how imagination side-steps
Half-witted nagging about 'National Identity'.

A deep-dyed Peter Pan-like reluctance to hold hands
With simpletons, or suffer fools gladly, prevents
What I don't believe. Day-dream tutorials,
With teachers you never meet, end up as this –
Whispers with the dead. It is greatly to be regretted.

Pushing fifty, though, it won't be difficult
To avoid it in future. I'm not sorry it happened.
It's a Scottish night. I look at the still Firth.
Avuncular and kindly wordless calm
Shines on the aesthetically mooned water.

Extra Helpings

In our primary school
Set lunch was the rule
Though in Scotland we call that meal 'dinner'.
We tucked in like starvelings,
Inchinnan's wee darlings,
And it didn't make thin children thinner.

But what I liked best
Was disliked by the rest,
Rice pudding with raisins and bloated sultanas,
Stewed fruit and dumplings
In big extra helpings
And hooray for first post-War bananas!
It was very good scoff
So I polished it off
A very dab hand with a spoon,
a spoon,
A very dab hand with my spoon.

Detested mashed turnip
Gave most kids the pip
While cabbage was much the same tale.
No shortage of roots, and no hardship of greens –
After mine I ate Harry's, then Elspeth's, then Jean's,
O a glutton for turnips and kail.
It was very good scoff
So I polished it off
A very dab hand with a fork,
a fork,
A very dab hand with my fork.

I used to be slim.
I used to be *slim*!
'Look!' they say now. 'There's at least *three* of him!'
To which I reply
With a daggerly eye,
'Well, that's better than three-quarters *you*!'
But my clothes don't fit
I'm fed up with it
And the sylph in me's guilty and blue.
> *Semolina and sago with jam,*
> > *with jam,*
> *Oh dear, what a pudding I am,*
> > *I am,*
> *Oh dear, what a pudding I am.*

But I'm longing for lunch
And something to munch
Though I wish it was back in that school
When the dinner-bell rings
And all good things
Await to be guzzled until I am happy and full.
Dear God, I'd die
For Shepherd's Pie
In 1949 or 1950
When the dinner-bell rings
And all good things
Draw children on the sniff and make then nifty.
> *It was very good scoff*
> *So I polished it off –*
> > *Oh dear, what a pudding I am,*
> > > *I am,*

Oh dear, what a pudding I am,
But a very dab hand with a spoon,
  a spoon,
And a very dab hand with a fork.

Preserve and Renovate

All day he's painted his fence, his gate,
As, yesterday, he sanded down the wood,
Replacing weather-rotted slats with good
Timber he'd cut. *Preserve and renovate.*
Do what you need to do, and do it now.
Mottoes like these explain fastidious hours
Spent tying up his borders' tasteful flowers –
No unexpected plants – the sheer know-how
Presented by the weedless path, squared hedge
And that blade-paddled, tended, watered lawn
Fit for a naked nymph to dance upon,
Though no nymph has, or would dare disoblige
The kirky vision of his husbandry
    Or get away with it,
  When, with his watchful pedantry,
He guards each moment of his dusk-grey privet.

He looked at me with almost-cross surprise
That I'd walked past his house four times today,
And yesterday, and though I tried to say
'Good morning' or 'Good afteroon', his eyes
Glanced with an elderly contempt at me
As if I'd trespassed on a sacred silence
Before he turned back to his mended fence
That he was painting white-as-white-could-be.

And he was right – my walks meant indolence
And curiosity; and he was wrong,
Because I saw in him ironic song
Echoing my dear father – an etched fragrance
From rubbed-down paint, glass paper, and the smell –
    Stooping in overalls,
  Doing, and doing the job well,
Then paint and brush and perfumes in the pulse.

That is my work, though he won't understand;
Nor could my father. It's what I do,
This risk of feeling, that the sweet and true
Might be preserved, presented by my hand
Among the many others who do this
For the same sake that is obedience to
Time and experience, for what is due
To being, to be life's accomplice.
Four times today, and yesterday, I saw
His patient, steady, careful labour plod
In imitation of his strait-laced God;
But he looked like my father. I could gnaw
At that facsimile for ever more;
    But I know who I lack,
  Not him, but that dead, distant doer
Who looked like him, who draws me back and back.

One Thing and Another

A fire was burning, and, as boys will do,
We raked that corner of the farm for dry
Combustible pickings, building it up
With sticks, tarpaulin rags, and waste roof-felt
Broken in slate-sized pieces that doused the blaze
To a flameless, stinking reek. One boy
Discovered a big can of old tractor drip.
It sat there for minutes while we dodged the smoke
In an eye-rubbing, coughing foxtrot.
I lifted up the petrol-smelly bucket.
At five feet from the spit and black smoulder,
Its flung, decanted arc ignited in
A bright industrial blast, a dangerous
Mid-twentieth-century bang. The can became
Too hot to handle. It was all live heat
For that split second before its gas hoof
Sent me up and back, singed and amazed,
Showing my ten hot blistered fingertips
In an involuntary flying pose.

Holding my daughter brings that feeling back
Through the sensation of her twist and kick,
Her hot will breaking free on a sudden
Obstinate, infant energy;
And I am up and back again to meet
That consequence of forty years ago
Ending its moment on this linked event,
Though what connects them, I don't know.

Early Autumn

Last month, by this same window, moist dusks
Closed the light slowly by summer curtains
And the eye had its space to go flying
Through glassy corners of sky, land and water.

Now it is dark and mid-September breathes
Numberless whispers. After blue sky,
Still Firth and summer's dry appearances,
Night is quick, with shivers at its edges.

Moths in the lampshades set to their *maudit*
Radiant, nocturnal manias, last gasps,
Powdery suicides on whirring wings.
They drop dead from electric interrogations.

My fingers smell of a soap that is new to me.
I should close windows, but aromatic fires
Linger from stubble burning all over Fife
And nothing's left of black daylight smoke.

An insect scribbles its white signature.
The letter 'a' can be seen through a veined wing.
Through 'a' the beginning of time can be seen,
A serpent's tongue licking around an apple.

Something begins in me; but I don't know
What it is yet. I shall try to find out.
It could be some sort of inhuman benevolence
Made of moth-powder, wings, smoke and soap.

A Game of Bowls

Hard to believe they were children once
Or in certain moods a lyrical triteness
Passes across the mind watching old men
Watching a game of bowls played by younger
Familiars on a day of green breezes.

That man's brother is named on the war memorial.
Two out of five are widowers and one
Went away and came back after forty years.
There were six but last week a man died
Reciting his nine-times table, sticking at

Nine-times-nine in an innumerate
Last few minutes of pillows and pain-killers.
Grandchildren rarely see them like this,
At their loose ends, one with a dog, another
Leaving his bench without a cheerio.

Or in certain moods it feels like half-a-tune
You can't put a name to, a spade's clink
On a stone, when you stand still, listening
To your ears and silence, then unseen children
Shouting from ten yards and many years away.

Just Standing There

It's a wooden bridge, an ordinary bridge,
A small one, on which I've stood many times,
Looking into the fast, earthy water, watching
Oddments sail by, rose-prunings from an upstream garden,
Twigs, litter, sometimes a flower-head, observing

Waterside botany immersed, dragged, but never drowned.
For years, though, I crossed the stream on my daily walk,
Ignoring that deep burn, or glancing at it.
Then I took to leaning on the timber parapet,
Staring into the fishless flood – or I've seen no fish
Ever in hundreds of quiet lookings, and if it dwindles
In summer, it is not by much, just enough
For an inch or two of bank to dry out, for a tuft
To lift its hair up from the tugging, onward rinse.
Insignificant, small, an ordinary wooden bridge,
It became a platform for a fifteen-minute staring
Into liquid muscle, a stamina that no one has
In mind or body – cliché of even little rivers
Or any patch of ground, stone, or man-outliving tree.
Commonplace as it is, it still took years to learn;
It took years to hear its several pitches of babble,
Watery lore encompassing tenderness and rage,
Always the same water, and never the same.
This is not an ordinary, small, wooden bridge,
I began to say to myself. It is my bridge.
It doesn't cross from reality to spirit,
But, in the middle, where I stand, leaning on the parapet,
Silent truth in me listens to a running giant
Let loose in unclocked liberty, as free as water
Drugged with its destination in the Firth and sea.
It's not my burn. Nothing like this is mine, it tells me.
And as for the bridge, it belongs to the municipality.
Reality is yours, and your spirit is your own.
Stand here, or anywhere, long enough, and you will learn
        that.
It's not the stream or the bridge; it's where I stand
At a precise spot of nowhere and timelessness
Within myself, a door I can go through and be invisible

In a room also invisible or from which I come back
Without memory other than languageless noise in the ears
Such as can be recalled clearly but never spoken.

Middle Age

It was around here in 1951
Where Pimples Pringle buried a dead rabbit
With my assistance in matters of ritual.
Either I recognize that stone
Or I want to badly enough to make it up.
We did it properly, with prayers, reverence,
A gully knife and a dessert spoon.
I catch myself rooting through the turf,
A mad archaeologist, for whom
Mid-twentieth-century cutlery means more
Then Celtic treasure or the Holy Grail.
If I find it, I'll run home with my secret trophy.
Nothing's left of our indignant melancholy
Other than this demented pathos looking for a spoon
In which to objectify itself. It's a big field,
For God's sake, but this is the exact spot –
I'm telling you, I *know*, I *remember* it!
So where, Pimples, did you drop the frigging spoon?
Why doesn't a big man-sized rabbit appear,
The God-of-all-the-Bunnies, and comfort me,
Stroke the back of my neck, present me with
An Electro-Plated Nickel Silver Spoon
And pin to my chest The Order of the Righteous Boy?
We sang 'Shall We Gather at the River?'
Which we'd heard in a movie starring John Wayne.
All those creatures, in graves dug by children.

Oh no, it's here; I'm telling you, I know...
Will all the people of the past come looking for me
As soon as it gets dark and I grow frightened?
I could sit here and find out. It'll be different at night.

Spanish Oranges

They strip so easily –
    I wonder why? –
Over- and under-frilly,
    No hook and eye.

Obstacle peel, you are
    Perfumed with south
And sweet as a mouth you are
    Mouth for my mouth.

Spherical word, it says
    Yes as I bite
Hispanic cabaret's
    Moorish delight.

Polyglot answers, *Si*'s
    Taste of *OK*
And a kissed, citric *Oui*'s
    Orange hooray.

Sun's nectareous south
    Sweetens my hands
And it drips from my mouth
    Plush Lorca-land's

Liquid guitars as night
    Dulcifies gender,
Succulent starlight,
    Lucid surrender.

Round fruit of the planet,
    Burst globe I hold,
The life and the love in it
    Beg to be told

Here in the north where I
    Guzzle and sip
Sensations that fructify
    Life on the lip.

Taste and the sense of it! –
    Plum, orange and peach,
Ripe melon's clean breast of it,
    Strawberry speech!

Number them all, such fruits
    Savour of life,
Love and the place of it, roots,
    Children and wife.

Garden Hints

Only a garden can teach gardening.
Better begin, then. Wilderness is best,
Raw ground for you to follow where it leads –
Don't bother if you haven't got the time –
Or else an ancient sanctuary, nurtured
Over centuries, from old tastes into yours.
Don't be enslaved by it. Instead, attend

With eager concentration to the place –
You live here and there's such a thing as change
Enabled by good work and husbandry.
Read what you can of histories of here
Until you sicken of their pain and woe,
Then you'll be happier with the present tense.
You'll find few chronicles of box-hedge, rose,
Cabbage, onion, beans, peas and artichoke.
Historians tend to miss the point of life's
Significant activities, labours
Truly of love, domestic devotions
For which reward is harvested improvements.
Few books on *these* subjects. Imagine them.
Elderly men might help with anecdotes
Raked from unselfish years of gardening
Such as you won't find in the *How To* books.
Live with the ground the way it is, and then,
Alert to quarters where sour winds arise,
Plant sheltering trees or build a wall
In keeping with the fabric of your parish.
Without advice from me, you'll have stretched out
On ground you like the look of, boulders which
You'll keep, stone roots to sit on and work round.
Astonishing your wife, you may have slept
Outdoors in a kapok bag, unused for years.
If she won't join you where tall grasses thrive,
Tell her you're thinking, or you feel the need
For outdoor, horticultural solitude.
Starting from scratch, that could be necessary –
A modern harvest, too, deserves its rites,
Spells, superstitions: plant a rowan tree.
A previous owner might have stamped the ground
With phoney gardening. With any luck

Gnomes and the brass flamingo will have gone
In the big van. Better for you, if he
Or she before you let the earth run wild,
Inviting your green surgery with spade,
Graip, hands and fingers, rooting out the rack,
Weeks of the ragged, earth-jammed fingernail.
Already tended in a style of new,
Then don't be lazy, make it style of you.
 Men, women, children, furniture, have gone;
Now you and yours repopulate a house.
So, labour warily. If a true hand
Tended the shape of it, your rose-tree will
Contain some of his spirit and the love
Between him and the woman who enjoyed
Cutting its flowers for her tabled vase.
Should she have been the gardener, you'll find
A feminine sensation in each rose.
Women who garden tend to leave their love
Wherever their gloved work's been done. Kneeling
Where women knelt, you'll feel the ghosts of love
Among undated plants, for gardens are
Intimate property, where previous claims
Share memories with present ownership.
Who, anyway, can own a tree, a flower,
Visiting butterflies, or a blade of grass?
In gardens you can sense the marriages
Of who lived here before, men and women,
Their private hours away without being gone.
The orphaned rose-tree mourned. Longevity! –
Work at your ground as if you mean to stay.
You'll measure life and time from that tall tree,
It's timber-ringed dendrochronology
Computing eras in its trunk, your own

Lifetime timetabled in its wooden clock.
Look after what you have. Don't be like me,
Besotted by arboreal mysteries,
Green legends and fluorescent narratives.
Don't turn your nose up at a climbing-frame,
Tree-house, a swing, or a gazebo where
Grannie can take her tea. A garden means
More than an introspective hour or two
For who's responsible for tending it.
It is a house turned inside out, a room
Higher than rooms, where sun shines, rain falls,
A room that's nothing like indoors, from where,
If you're lucky, you can see for miles.
     Hortus becomes a virtue if you can
Believe in what a garden teaches you.
Make it a work of love, a work of man
Befriended by the sociable and true,
Where children leave their toys, and wives their books.
Your house outside, a children-shouted shade
Where ball games batter shrubs, and little boys
Put beetles in bug-boxes, toddlers chase bees,
And the gardener's bad back in springtime
Becomes a family joke – although domestic,
Still keep a patch for mystery, where briars
Protect Priapus from the prurient
And shield his lover from offended eyes
Intent on newest things, not native classic.
For only those who know what gardens mean
Obey a garden's deities, or know
Transferred humanity has made them so
And that they always were protectors of
Days of loveliness, when flowers and fruits
Ripen according to the gardener's toil.

You'll know your gods are there when children play
Or friends are gathered on a summer's day;
And if you have a lawn,
Let it be grass kept sweet for walking on.

Long Ago

In a house I visited when I was young
I looked in through a partly opened door.
An old man sang 'Long Ago and Far Away'
To a rocking-horse, a friend's grandfather
Whose first-born son was lost at sea
Half-a-century before
In a ship whose name I have forgotten.

Whenever that sad song is played or sung
I'm in that house again, by that same door.
A woman tugs my sleeve. 'Come away,'
She says. 'Leave him alone.'
He sings, but he's no longer there.
The rocking-horse is rocking like the sea.
Ocean is everywhere
And the room is wind and rain.

Saturday's Rainbow

It happened that I saw it paint itself
In light and liquid. Sky
Turned into art. Original
Cloud-Constables emerged
To make new moments when

The eye's in love with wonder.
'Go on, then, break my heart,' I dared
To the big window as I watched
Sudden, shaded radiance declare
Its moist lustre, its big phenomena
Vivid with wet physics, working together
To arch across the Tay and link
Tentsmuir to Monifieth
Where people walked along the beach
At each bright, leaking root of it
Straining to hold the curve, driving each hue
Beyond the commonplace, towards perfection.
Those distant people disappeared in it
Or else they found
Intimate, legendary treasure on
Kaleidoscopic sand.

Then it began to break.
Its cylinders decayed. It vanished bit by bit –
Violet, indigo and blue,
Green, yellow, orange and red.
If only how we live could be as true
In our arrivals and departures as
A rainbow comes and goes...
It left its light-print on the conifers,
Its seven-coloured, seven-heavened smears;
And after seven flourishes, the sky
Departed in an optical goodbye.

'Scenic Tunnels'

Niagara Falls, Canada, 7 April 1992

Portals open on
Cold, wet cremation.
Phenomenal essence
Thunders constantly
Against the eye –
It never stops –
And is decreated
Over and over
At the same speed's
Roaring velocity.
Infinite weight
Turns into air,
Water, haze, and blink,
But as if fire also
Plays its elemental role
In this droughtless wonder:
It is so absent
That you think of it
And you think of it
And you see white fire.
Subterranean winds
Whoosh in the rock.
Downward momentum –
It looks like ice,
Arctic power's
Venerable brawn
Crazed by falling,
The boiling bergs,
That sort of wonder –
Not one of seven

But of very many,
Some of them mine,
Some yours, some those
Of she who died
A few hours later
Outside Erie,
For I don't forget.
It is all of
Twenty-seven years ago.
With this photograph
(Three weeks later)
I hold summer
1965.
My thumb's pulse tumbles
Its own Niagara
And my eyes bubble
Looking at Maggie,
Lesley (both dead),
In printed mist's
Light-written white-blue.

Thunder, lightning,
Ice and thunder
Ice in the eye
By the cold furnace
And the yellow macs,
Everyone like children
And the blind children
Who are here, listening
Smiling as the blind smile,
Listening, unafraid.
Spectacular noise

Rumbles, perhaps
The voice of God.

God forgive me.
My old self strains
Against this new one.
The tunnel's end
Shows no light, only
Natural wrath,
White turmoil, force
Into which men cut,
Tunnelled, engineering
Forbidden glimpses
Into the heart.
Ice-smoke. Water-fire.
Horror of self.
Close a door on it.

from THE DONKEY'S EARS

PART ONE

V

We've wound our watches back. Britannic time
Inched on this cruising of the hemisphere
Reverses me by five knots back, my dear,
To you, to comfort and indoor sublime.

English, Self-Taught lies open and unread.
It's been a day of sweat and damaged boats.
'War news' goes round in rumoured anecdotes –
Misleading gossip mouthed by the misled.

I've been dozing, remembering yesterday
Lunching among the maps. Our Admiral's
Cigar smoke settled on its lazy whorls;
His map-room's sky dulled with Havana grey,

Clouding the gobal charts, while, like a ghost,
His spectral steward wiped the cognac stains
Ringed in wet liquor on the numbered mains,
Indelible off the Korean coast,

All eighteen thousand miles of buts and ifs
Away. His hand slid past – starched, spotless cuff! –
Mopping the sea-miles in the *Suvorov*,
Wiping the brandied bays and ash-flecked reefs.

VI

Lulled by moonlight; like warm autumn, it was,
Deep on the grassy plains, or watching stars
From windows looking out on city squares
When poplars rustle and the cafés close.

These airing stokers long for solid ground,
Cursing conscription and geography.
Heart-breaking moonlight bleaches on the sea.
A Russian navy takes the long way round.

Three thousand tons a day – they shovel coal
Down in their hot and grunting odium
And sing to moonlight with a lyric from
Old Russia's anachronistic soul.

A clockhand searchlight drops its silver on
Small waves that shatter it. From *Suvorov*
I watch these little lights float, thinking of
Your bird-crumbs scattered on a frosted lawn.

VII

All Europe claims a Scythian wanderlust
Impels our fleet towards the yellow East,
A sea-hoofed modern Mongolian beast
Armada'd in the Tsardom's permafrost.

Our enemy is everything that floats.
I stood on the afterbridge, hot from below,
And watched the needle searchlights stitch and sew
A fantasy of eight torpedo boats.

Guns flashed and sucked the air from ears and lungs,
Each white blink showing us how we might die
In nightmare, up-to-date mortality.
I left the bridge, rung by vibrating rung,

And from the afterdeck, I saw our lights
Rake up an empty smack, then hesitate
On gear and tackle, a civilian net,
As sitting targets in our gunners' sights.

Even a half-Lieutenant whom I've seen
Read treasonable pamphlets in his bunk
Went mad with bloodlust on the Dogger Bank
Prepared to die serving a six-inch gun.

If I'd been diligent with *English, Self-Taught*,
I might have had a name to put in this;
But it went down in white analysis
In the illiterate but polyglot

Atrocity of sea, blood on its deck
As up its stern heaved. Its legal light
Shone deep as garnets set against the night,
Red, red for 'Stop', that helpless rhetoric.

Our 'modern' fleet, iron arithmetic,
Metallurgy and engineering law,
Go down in scandal. A man beside me saw
Two fishermen hold up four half-dead haddock.

VIII

Aurora's holed below her waterline –
Imaginary, midnight Japanese!
Our guns were real, but not our enemies...
An empire, at its zenith, in decline!

In a gun-silence, the black *Suvorov*
Steams for the East, with priests and holy relics
While half the crew carries a crucifix,
Though it's a chaplain's had his hands blown off!

But now the wardroom dogs chase champagne corks
Across the floor, and bits of card on string.
Our midshipmen are remanoeuvring
Last night's 'attack' with sugar cubes and forks.

Pale stewards from the wardroom stoves serve tea
While officers of guns boast of the rate
Their magazines served shells up to them at,
Their ears cocked to obsessive gunnery.

I sit in a corner, my love, my glass
A perfect image of a small, clear sea.
Old hands at this game, we sit quietly,
And toast ourselves in vodka's veritas.

IX

So far, so far to sail. And then, for what?
I think it is the century compels us.
An antique nineteenth century expels us
And time's the mystery in which we're caught,

The web of 'progress' (meaning bigger guns).
And me, a poet! Sophie, be delighted
I work to hope I'll hear myself recited
After my labours on these damaged tons.

[PART TWO]

III

Hamburg-Amerika's coal-laden tramps
Heave-to alongside, hull to buffered hull,
Our hireling colliers with their bunkers full.
A messman sells me Spanish postage stamps.

Crafty for profit, but illiterate.
Unnecessary officers relax
With a haircut, shoes raised to the bootblack's
Duster, its soothingly civilian pat.

'Good as a turn ashore,' Ignatzius says,
Posing a polished shoe. Leontiev's mad –
The barber soused him with the wrong pomade.
On deck, the creak and swing of the Temperleys.

Four officers they've blamed for firing on
Innocent trawlers on the Dogger Bank
Go off to walk the diplomatic plank –
Scapegoats our admiral hangs his bungling on.

But Rozhestvensky, too, 's packed Klado off,
That self-conceited bore and 'strategist',
Know-nothing self-styled expert, bad hand at whist,
Taking his pedantry and nasty cough.

The water-sprinting swans on Vigo Bay
Go where they go, into an anywhere
Sheltered for them, pair by domestic pair.
In nature there's no nationality.

IV

Nocturnal clearings and Hispanic stars,
The asterisks of God, an opulent
Notation of the sky, as in Tashkent –
Remember? – when, like paired astronomers

We saw the stars of Allah shine on us
And kissed and heard erotic harness bells
Affirm two honeymooning infidels –
Welcoming, Arabic, euphonious.

The things I noticed then and do not now,
Or can't, or notice now but didn't then –
South and disabled off the coast of Spain,
A Russian Sinbad in his armoured dhow!

Autumn-near-winter, in 1904,
My year of atlases come true, a year
Since Kazakhstan. I close down on Tangier,
Corsair and Barbary, its Moorish shore,

And I sense you, Sophie, and hold your hand
In a dreamt aroma as the Prophet's roar
Growls on the October surf, a metaphor
Describing Africa to Samarkand.

                    V

Haunted by British cruisers, *Oryol* collapsed
Around the strain of its unanswering wires,
Jamming its steering-gear. Nelsonian squires
Laughed as they watched our seamanship eclipsed

By their nimble patterns, our lumbering fleet
Black and lemon-yellow to their lean, warlike
Athletic grey, ruthless as Caspian pike,
Trafalgared, thorough, turning their sea-neat

Figures around us. Rozhestvensky cursed
Reservists for their landlocked innocence.
Men tremble in the forethought of such omens
Of ocean-war in which they're unrehearsed

Especially as they know their Admiral's
No genius when it comes to battle-tactics
Though very good at Romanov tyrannics,
And seeing right in wrong, and true in false.

VI

Ten years of Nicholas! Hurrah! Hurrah!
His anniversary on *Suvorov*
Cheers up our loyalty's official love,
Logged thus, as 'off the coast of Africa'.

Vodka below-decks and champagne above
As officers and drunken ratings share
Our servile State's conservative despair
Nursed on the regal lap of Romanov.

Cheers from the deck of sister *Borodino*
Draw our attention from imperial lunch.
Ignatzius chews, and, coughing on his munch,
He says, 'Pray for Napoleonic snow.'

VII

A lemon wind blew from the citrus groves
Before light rain. It's a great event
To a domestic man, this whiff of scent
From the planet's Moroccan alcoves.

Tonight I'm slave to my imagination.
All day I calculated, sketched, and dug
In Napier's tables in a dialogue
With facts and answers. Mathematician

To battleships, repairer of their faults,
I hate the sea's wrinkled mechanics, its
Full force of weathered sames and opposites
Rearing its only element, its salts

Ground in its seabed quarries. All night long
Our bands played as the men competed for
Prizes for fastest coaling, each competitor
A muscled serf to roubles and to song.

I sent a wire, Sophie, but no answer yet
Tapped over the blue Europe between us.
Telegraphed Morse-code's waltz-time's blurt and buzz
Finds me queued for you. Some get, most don't get

Telegraphed billets-doux, but scribbled joy
Sometimes, in the telegraphist's panache
As he decodes each cryptic dot and dash,
Shoves up his specs, and shouts it – 'It's a boy!'

[PART FOUR]

VI

Unsounded waters and an imperfect chart
Reduce the fleet to sluggishness, one knot
In line ahead, the speed of soundsmen's thought,
Serving their navigators' prudent art.

Verse, too, is cautious, as it finds its way
Through depths and shallows, always looking for
Celestial heights above, the ocean floor
Below, the highs and lows of life, its play

With sorrows, joys and griefs, its ups and downs,
Its all-too-celebrated crests and troughs.
Enough of metaphor! That stuff's for toffs
Who went to school on it and who'd pronounce –

Ignatzius *would*! – my feeble verse too cautious,
Too much an engineer's spannered response
To everyday emotions and sensations
While short on the artistic and audacious.

Golovko found my jottings and *protested*.
'I served a master once. *He* was a scribbler.
His hair fell out! I warn your worship. Sir,
As well as bald, he got himself *arrested*!'

I swore the man to silence. We get on
Better than most paired officers and servants.
He neither touts, nor drops conspicuous hints,
Nor rifles through my cabin when I'm gone –

I'd left my notebook open, having been forced
To run to an emergency last night.
I wasn't *sure* that he can read and write –
And that last piece unfinished and half-versed! –

But now I know he can, because he said
(Can you believe it?) that his wife, too
(It startles me!) is Sophie! And it's true.
He showed a letter from her, and he read

It out – perfectly! – then signed off with her name.
We shook hands and embraced in tears for this
Coincidence and the name on a kiss.
Master and servant, whose wives' names are the same!

Later, called out to fix another ship,
I worried: Could good old Golovko be
A policeman and his supervision me?
Such times, that master-servant comradeship

Attracts suspicious thoughts! I feel ashamed
But wonder if that man who lost his hair
(If not fictitious) cursed his unaware
Embrace for two wives virtuously named.

Shallow seas continue, and, with dunting hulls,
Damage, repairs. – Our navigators are
Better at distance and a charted star
Than close-up, intimate, perfected skills.

Golovko with his letter, though – like mine,
It's old, from Libau ... Men, reading old letters,
Servants, ratings, and their so-called 'betters',
There being no new ones for our paper shrines...

Handwriting on the eye is such a pleasure,
Sophie, that it's too hard to say why
A temperament of hand delights the eye,
Read, re-read, stared at, at our lonely leisure.

A different sort of speech from the Admiral's
Emotional calls to God, Country and War,
Russia, Destiny and the great Emperor!
I sit by this bug-beaded lamp and feel my pulse.

[PART FIVE]

XXV

Colonial society, my dear,
Would drive you mad as these French women are.
Despite their resolute *petit bourgeois*
Routines and calling cards on this frontier

Where stays and millinery make no sense,
They still insist on tennis parties, dressed
In all the finery of the self-possessed,
Decked out in a *Parisienne* pretence

That fashion counts in Madagascar where
Tropical heat, rain and mud, alternate with
Drought and dust, and where slow or sudden death
Are facts of which these ladies are aware –

Disease, rebellions, or from sheer despair.
I pity merchants' and officials' wives
Here, in this heat – a squandering of lives
For empire and the chance of Otherwhere.

A Madame Bovary of Nossi-Bé
Flirted with officers. Her husband complained
To the Admiral, but the comedy's stained
With gossip, for I heard the other day

That the Governor's wife has laid the blame
On would-be Emma for our cancelled shore leave.
How like provincial Russia! They deceive
Themselves with the exchange of petty shame

When it's well-known that heavy gambling debts
Run up in Nossi-Bé's straw-roofed casino
Forced Admiral Rozhestvensky to say 'No'
To card games and to primitive roulette

Where officers and men were being skint,
Including me – toot-toot, my dear – Mammon
Being served with all the thrills of backgammon,
In my case, ending up as semi-solvent.

A drama, then, of gossip, thwarted lust.
Torpor, and turpitude, games for high stakes,
Say by themselves that anything that slakes
Ennui's almighty thirsts, or breaks the crust

That boredom bakes around us, will be seized
With hope or gratitude. I understand it,
This need for excess, for extortionate
Pleasures, and I take part; but I'm not eased

As much by gambling as I used to be.
Remember those slow, snow-beamed winter nights
In Yuri's long-windowed house, those Muscovites
At cards, gambling obsessively, elegantly? –

Well, it's not like that! It's more addiction
To the uncertainty that hangs over us
Than social pleasure or a prosperous
Hand of good luck. We're turning into fiction.

XXVI

Vanilla, coffee, leather, coconut oil,
Hardwoods, lemurs for European zoos...
When I'm back home with you, I'll write *The Cruise
Of the Second Pacific Squadron*, spoil

A dozen reputations and be a bore
At dinners. I'll be *really* irritating.
I'll be appalling. I'll be *excruciating*.
Among the windbags, I'll be excelsior.

I'll open with, 'Yes, back in nineteen-five
With the Fleet, holed up in stinking Nossi-Bé...
Did I ever tell you I'd been down that way?
Yes? Ah! It's down to luck I'm still alive,

'You know, after what I went through down there
In the southern seas. Yes, I've done it all,
Been round the world, and been in battle...'
– Dear God, I must be dreaming! – 'Everywhere.

'I've been everywhere. Seen so many things.
Wonders! Strange creatures of both sea and land
But here's a story I can't understand –
The sailor who stole the church offerings.

'For the life of me, I can't get the hang
Of why he did it. But he did. Confessed,
Indeed. Ashamed. Full of remorse. "No rest
For me, ever," he said. "While those nuns sang,

'"I nicked their box. I'm sorry, sir," he said
Before the special court convened to try
That strange young man, whose tearful, soulful sigh
Shocked me with mystery, his face, his head,

'Sombre with ruin, a most sensitive,
Almost artistic handsomeness. "I drink,"
He said defiantly. "I live to drink.
I beg of you. I don't deserve to live."

'"I'm pleased to hear it," said the President.
"Assuming that the Admiral will ratify
Its judgement, this court rules that you shall die
By firing squad. And that's your punishment."

'I did *not* agree. It didn't get *my* vote.
You gasp? You think it harsh, or think me wrong?
It hardly matters now. I wasn't strong.
On every battleship, torpedo-boat,

'Cruiser, transport, or whatever, officers
Drank like fish, and they didn't have to steal
To do so. They just ran up a big bill
In the wardroom, and that man called them "Sirs".

'The officer presiding, he drank, too.
He drank, and he was drinking when he judged
That petty theft, and he wouldn't be budged.
Indeed, he drank as much, or more, than you' –

And I'll look at someone. 'Forget the death.
I was ashamed, watching the firing squad's
Trembling reluctance to perform as God's
Accessories, takers of life and breath.

'On the first command to fire, they all missed.
That strange young man, he smiled, and held his face,
Somehow – as if he welcomed his disgrace.
It was appropriate that they were pissed.

'The second volley, too ... The officer
In charge ordered that *all* rifles be loaded
With live rounds, and the firing squad was goaded
And yelled at. It responded with "Yes, Sir!"

'Slobbered and slurred, a kind of mockery,
And there was something almost like tenderness
In how their bullets this time didn't miss
Their handsome target. But what was his story?

'It's the mops I hear, swabbing the gundeck clean,
Washing the blood away, the human stains,
Twelve bullets' worth, heartblood, and the spilled brains.
It's the mops I hear. Do you know what I mean?'

And then I'll go quiet. I'll sink in my chair.
There are those who'll think it's all for effect
And quite beneath their hardnosed intellect.
Later, I'll jump up and shout, *'I've been there!'*

[PART SIX]

XVII

Yesterday was autumn, but today it's spring.
Who'd cease to be astonished by this planet,
The definite, the known, the infinite?
Science comforts me with its surprising

Discoveries, the way poetry can't
Get through to fact, or the material
Knowledge of substance, true, useful, real,
Workable improvements that cantos can't

Deliver, and never will – that's *their* glory.
A poem measures nothing, but can cure
Diseased time, and make the uncertain sure.
The way a child asks, 'Tell me a story!' . . .

The way a story answers to a child's
Deepest interest! . . . Ah, I remember how
I read of snow, before, I saw the snow
For the first time fall on the Muscovian fields,

And dreamt I was dreaming, or else I thought
I might be thinking it, that rhyme of white
With all the wide world on that moonlit night.
What did I learn that night, what was I taught

Far from Tashkent, my mother holding me?
'See, Eugen,' – she said me in German – 'There!
I think of snow as poetry and prayer.
One day, my son, I'll take you to the sea.'

[PART NINE]

V

I'm now prepared for battle, having stowed
All my belongings in my cabin trunk –
My souvenirs from where I've been, much junk
From Africa, dead clothes, and the yellowed

Sheets of your letters to me, photographs
Of you, and this in my battered jotter
Well-wrapped in oilskins to protect from water
In case we're sunk. Good old Ignatzius laughs

At my precautions, for I've told him that
I've passed my night-watch writing verse to you.
I had to tell him. But he said he *knew*.
'I know. I've always known. Golovko spat,

'Then rubbed his spit into the quarterdeck
Before he cleared his throat, and told me he
Was very worried for you, writing poetry
All night. He thought you were mad, or a wreck,

'Or cracking up. He can read, and he knew
That what he watched you writing was a poem.
That's Old Russia for you! Blow me if I'm
Indifferent to my officers and crew,

'But old Golovko sobered me, because
Although he could read it, and he could see
That what you'd written down was poetry,
He *didn't* read it, but just saw what it was.

'I've far too much to do today, or else
I'd offer you a connoisseur's critique.
My God, an engineer! Well, you've a cheek . . .
I'll read it later, Vladivostok, Hell's

'Library, or wherever we fetch up.'
Dear friend, Ignatzius! Yes, I'll let him read
My amateur epistles' scribbled screed
On absence, water, love, and the far Europe

Which, I'm convinced, will suffer this century
As no other. Suffering's relative –
Of course it is. I wish I'd time to live
And learn more, but I'm stuck in penury

As far as time's concerned. Our Admiral's
Hell-bent on battle in the narrow straits
Between Korea and Japan. He hates
Japan, the Japanese, and now he drills

His Staff in loathing for our enemy.
He shouts and barks at us – '*You must despise
Our dwarfy foe, those men with little eyes!*'
He's set our course for death and infamy.

I'll have to hurry. Our unarmed transports
Will leave us soon for Shanghai, and with mail
If I can finish this before they sail
To booze and safety and the sexual sports

For which the city's famous. Not for me!
My uniform's been pressed, so if I die
I'll be well dressed, gold cufflinks, black bow-tie,
Wing collar, dressed to meet the horrid sea.

from THE YEAR'S AFTERNOON

The Year's Afternoon

As the moment of leisure grows deeper
I feel myself sink like a slow root
Into the herbaceous lordship of my place.
This is my time, my possessive, opulent
Freedom in free-fall from salaried routines,
Intrusions, the boundaryless tedium.
This is my liberty among trees and grass
When silence is the mind's imperfect ore
And a thought turns and dallies in its space
Unhindered by desire or transactions.
For three hours without history or thirst
Time is my own unpurchased and intimate
Republic of the cool wind and blue sea.
For three hours I shall be my own tutor
In the coastal hedge-school of grass furniture.
Imaginary books fly to my hand
From library trees. They are all I need.
Birdsong is a chirp of meditative silence
Rendered in fluttered boughs, and I am still,
Very still, in philosphical light.
I am all ears in my waterside aviary.
My breath is poised for truth to whisper from
Inner invisibilities and the holiness
Venturesome little birds live with always
In their instinctive comforts. I am shedding
The appetites of small poetry and open to
Whatever visits me. I am all eyes
When light moves on water and the leaves shake.
I am very still, a hedge-hidden sniper
In whose sights clarified infinity sits
Smiling at me, and my skin is alive

To thousands of brushed touches, very light
Delicate kisses of time, thought kisses,
Touches which have come out of hiding shyly
Then go back again into the far away
Surrender they came from and where they live.
Perfecting my afternoon, I am alert to
Archival fragrances that float to me
Unexplained over the world's distances.
This is my time. I am making it real.
I am getting rid of myself. This is my time.
I am free to do whatever I wish
In these hours, and I have chosen this
Liberty, which is an evanishment
To the edges of breath, a momentary
Loss of the dutiful, a destitute
Perchance, a slipping away from life's
Indignities and works into my freedom
Which is beyond all others and is me.
I am free to do as I like, and do this;
I sink like a slow root in the name of life
And in the name of what it is I do.
These are my hours of 1993.
Ears, eyes, nose, skin and taste have gone.
For a little while I shall be nothing and good.
Then other time will come back, and history.
I shall get up and leave my hiding place,
My instinctive, field-sized republic.
I shall go home, and be that other man.
I shall go to my office. I shall live
Another year longing for my hours
In the complete afternoon of sun and salt.

My empty shoes at the bedside will say to me,
'When are we taking you back? Why be patient?
You have much more, so much more, to lose.'

T. E. Lawrence at The Ozone
in memoriam George Kendrick

If Bridlington appears the sort of place
No one of consequence would linger in
Beyond the close of business, it's not true.
Here T. E. Lawrence messed about in boats
And, once demobbed, was put up at The Ozone.
What this has to do with you, George, old friend,
Might be just one of those mysteries of verse
We used to talk about. It's Bridlington,
Of course it is, and Lawrence's lost Ozone,
As well as where you were born, a place you liked,
And I liked too, on that day together,
Drinking beer, eating fish, listening to
Your anecdotes of Suez, teaching, verse,
As you unwinded, and we talked about
T. E. Lawrence and the vanished hotel.
No longer in the *Yellow Pages*, gone
Into the guest-house annals, second-hand
Emporia where knapery and cutlery
Circulate among passed-on furniture, plates,
Cups and saucers, I think about Lawrence
In a lost room at the end of his service
On his last days here, writing his letters,
Preparing for ununiformed existence,
A few years more to polish his enigma.
Down at the harbour, through a smell of fish,

A scent gets through, distilled in Araby,
Sandalwood, coffee, frankincense and myrrh,
And someone senior to him saying 'Sir'
Split seconds after he had slipped away
Into the ether in his demob suit
Heading to destiny from destiny
On his Homeric motorcycle.
Dear George, my memory of you, somehow
Or other (such *is* the mystery) is here,
Too – Bridlington harbour, talk, fish, and beer
Remembered in a sensation of *always*
And shared *Gauloises*, walking along the pier
Speaking of life and poetry, the ways
In which a line or two can say so much
Existence. Old friends being philosophical!

Art is Wonderful

Now that you've found us, strip. Yes, naked. Please.
No one can see you. No, you aren't 'safe'.
Yes, everything, including socks and shoes.

You're feeling humble? Walk into Room One.
Before you ask, the man you see there is
Well and truly stuffed, and no effigy.

He's an oboeist-ideologue of 1937.
Beside him in the glass case you can see
Corrected flutes and censored violins,

A Red tuba and an Aryan clarinet.
That pickled larynx in the little jar
Belonged to a dictator's diva.

The room itself 's conflated from thirteen
Bunkered boudoirs, while that gramophone
Raved with sophisticated folklore as

Its owner plotted on strategic maps
And inspiration dug millions of graves.
That, as you know, is what you're listening to –

Countless busy amateur undertakers.
National epics are death certificates.
It's a lucky country that doesn't have them.

Room Two contains unpublished libraries,
Secret editions, and artists' farewell notes
Spotted with tears. Hence the noiseless fountain.

In spaces between silent anthems, you'll hear
Solitary shots in the back of the neck
And the consciences of conscripts in firing squads.

No, nothing in Room Three. Nothing. Except
An exile's sigh. Nothing at all. Nothing
Other than nocturnal human noise, farts,

Feet shuffling in dust, a child's cry,
A scream out of an unforgotten rape
Trying to find its home in a footnote.

In Four, however, study the withered bouquets
On the wall hung also with ballet shoes.
Listen to all those recorded bravos.

In Five, observe demented gargoyles
Dismantled from Party architecture.
Now you can understand why nakedness

Means something as you stand before
Mass-murderers portrayed in lousy oils
Or the once ubiquitous office photographs.

Backbiting poets turned each other in
To cultural police, and here you have them
Preserved in Six. Yes, more than you thought.

Those were the days of the Denounced Concerto
And states of mind that led directly to
Drudgery, death, and through the guarded gates.

Room Seven, therefore, is dedicated to
Honesty, fidelity, and humiliation.
We convey this through sub-zero temperatures,

The smell of sweat, ordure, and decomposition.
It is all written down. Nothing is lost.
Be warned by this. Your microphoned ambition

Gives off much the same aroma, and so, too, does
Detestable fame-footwork smack of the same
Dishonest, selfish choreography.

And now, enjoy the spectacle of The Arts
In their moods of 'Health Through Strength',
'A Day Down on the Collective Farm',

'With the Heroic Construction Crews at X',
'I Painted This to Make Lots of Money'.
Room Eight is complicated but depressing.

Room Nine is just meant to remind you.
Hence the exhibits of unsculpted stone,
Colours, pencils, paper, and instruments,

Alphabets, tools, wood, the notes of the scales,
An empty stage, Comedy, and Tragedy.
Room Nine is the Unvarnished Truth. Love it.

Room Ten is your room. Do not leave the room
As you find it. Make your mark on its walls.
It is not defacement to write on them.

It is up to you what you choose.
Why do you need to ask? LIBERTY. ART.
BEAUTY. TRUTH. They're all lying to hand.

They're charms against terror's arithmetic.
They'll preserve you from stupidity.
They'll make your life difficult, your work true.

Leave by the door ahead of you. Your clothes
Will be found where you left them. Hurry.
No. You can't come back. Don't attempt it.

Be quick. Another is waiting.
No, as I said, you can't return here.
Do I need to say everything twice?

Another is waiting. Another is always waiting.
You chose. Don't complain of your life.
There are no second chances. That is the point.

Three Poets

I

It was a very bad year for the deaths of poets –
Norman MacCaig, Sorley MacLean, and George Mackay
    Brown.
Then everybody move up one? No, it's
All drop down and kiss the ground
For the lyric scourge of hypocrites,
The bardic master, the voice of an Orcadian town.

Disturbed anthologies! *Memento mori* –
George Mackay Brown, Norman MacCaig, and Sorley
    MacLean.
They died in the same year! A tripled cry
In metrical, thrice-measured sound
Praises the biggest man of Skye,
The earl of Hamnavoe, and the prince of the humane.

Three great men lost within one lousy year! –
Sorley MacLean, George Mackay Brown, Norman MacCaig.
Words feel disordered and they can't cohere
Unless to toast truly crowned
Dead verse-heroes, but not in beer –
No, by *George, Norman, and Sorley*, we won't be vague!

II

Norman, when asked, 'Norman, do you smoke?'
Answered politely with his polished joke –
'Almost professionally.' Norman, I do, too,
As you knew, and as you said was 'good for me'
Although I'm not so sure. I'm not like you.
A lung of mine *barks*, and it scans *spondee*.

Norman, when asked, 'Norman, do you drink?'
Thought for a second, and said, 'Do I *think*?'
Then when the malt was poured, the hostess said,
'Would you like something in it?' Norman stared.
'Another tilt of *that* pure thoroughbred
Glen Grant, and water, please, and then I'm watered.'

Norman, a handsome man, adored ladies,
Who adored him. He loved the Hebrides.
He loved Assynt, warblers, stonechats, dry-stane dykes,
Small lochs with herons – so, put it about,
He was a man of more likes than dislikes –
Friends, ladies, swans, toads, cormorants, and trout.

What Norman *didn't* like, Norman *detested*
With wit such as could get a man arrested –
For cut-price academics, pedants, bores,
Or sanctimonious swine – his lethal ire! –
Or frauds, or politicians who cause wars.
Lyric intelligence, but ringed with fire!

III

'Keep left', he used to say, 'Keep left', meaning
'Get off my right-hand side, it's deaf',
As well as something political, as if
I might have faltered in my own leaning
To the left side of intellect, the left
Frontier and margin of mind's craft and drift.

In Austria – Sorley, Eddie, Liz, and me,
British Council-ing – three poets trembled for
Sorley, that old 'don't talk about the war'

Punctilio, knowing what will be will be,
And, knowing Sorley, what you could predict –
Six feet and eighty years of self-respect,

His warrior Gaelic verse, its ancestry
In a thousand stories, valorous big blades
Swinging through battles, feuds and cattle raids,
And no hint of remorse or sophistry.
Pre-supermarket, Sorley, you'd no choice
Other than Gaelic's unsurrendered voice.

Like Lovat's soldiers speaking Gaelic over
Open radio, your language fell on ears
Still puzzled after forty-something years
By melodies that sounded like an undercover
Elusive code, a tongue no German knew,
And music, not the meaning, getting through.

I like to think of one of Rommel's men
Listening in to Gaelic conversation
Through earphones in the desert, listening in,
A wondering philologist, his pen
Jotting phonetics, then, closing his eyes,
Hears sea and islands and Atlantic skies.

IV

Your fragrance finished, but your love and lore
Survive in your inscribed and lovely verse.
I never met a man, George, who knew more
Truth than you did, or felt less for commerce.

Iconic, weathered, Nordic, proud, and calm...
You were your own epoch. You were your own.
Your sculpted lyric and your runic psalm
Came from a world before the telephone,

Modernity, TV, and apparatus –
From your domain of faith's handwritten craft,
Orcadian sky, Orcadian afflatus,
The truths and histories you epitaphed.

V

Depleted poetry! The tides still ebb and flow,
Rose-clouds pinken, hills are white with year-end snow.
But ah! the naked birch trees and the frosted grass,
The weather-sorrow measured on the weatherglass,
The winking lights, diminished day, the river flowing,
A robin on the climbing-frame, the darkness growing
As nineteen ninety-six gets put away and time
Aches to the measures of posterity and rhyme.

A large subtraction from our triple-tongued sublime!
Come, we should listen to the shadows, to the light,
To peat becoming ash in the lyrical night
As it darkens to deepest splendour, as flames climb
In the lum and the indoor pine's baubles swing and chink
In a strange draught. Come, friends, it is time now to drink
To three poets. It is time to sit quietly and read,
Hearing them speak their lines, those whom we succeed,

Our chiefs of men, our leaders in the spirit of us,
Those whom we loved for showing us the wit of us.
Drink, then, with a full heart, with gratitude, saying
Their poetry aloud as if we are praying
To the Muse of our country, asking her to guide us,
To keep us true and triple, not to divide us
Into pathetic factions set on matricide.
Lady, guide us. Re-teach us dignity and pride.

Come, friends, it is time now to drink to three poets.
Let us raise our glasses to those who strengthened our wits.
Come, friends, let us drink to our nation's finest men.
Let us drink to them. Then let us drink to them again.

Woodnotes

Looking into a wood, the mind gets lost
In complicated sameness, on and on.
Senses grow green and wooden. My own ghost
Waves from ground-misted ferns, and then it's gone
In half the time it takes to blink. Mind, leaf,
Life, mist, stop together in the soft clock
Within me, caught on thorns of disbelief
And welcome, as a life's *tick-tock, tick-tock*
Delivers its involuntary beats
Into an unthinned forest's olive light
Clammy with earth-locked rain, high summer heat's
Low airlessness, dusk dwindling into night.

A selfish, inner, pleasurable fright
Lasting no time at all, or man-shaped mist,
Botanic fog, a kind of second-sight,
A trick of light that says I, too, exist –
Whatever incommunicable threat
Stood in the ferns and waved – knowable fate,
Momento mori or my spirit's sweat
Evaporating – I saw my duplicate.
Abject but happy with the sight I saw
I stood and sniffed the stink of my remorse
Flow from my years and deeds, fault laced with flaw,
A silent, sniffing, waving, grinning discourse.

Silence like music that must not be played,
A score that must be read with the body posed
At a forbidden instrument, dismayed
Hands locked above potential music closed
To its performance – play it in the mind,
An abstract symphony releasing real
Ethical harmonies until they're signed
As what you cannot say but what you feel.
In a birdless forest where no fresh winds blow
I saw my other stand among the ferns
And what I didn't know I got to know
And what I learned is what a dead man learns.

Oblivion at an instant's open door –
The green of it, my whole life running past –
And then I was back again, the forest's floor
Greener than ever in the hemmed-in vast
Confinedness of the wood. I waved back
At where I'd been while being where
I'd seen him/me. A leaf dripped and a black
Defoliated tree creaked like my chair
But quietly so that only I could hear
(Or so I thought) its phrases of dead wood
Dismiss themselves; but what they meant was clear –
Revise your life, and use your solitude.

Exilic, but the root still strong and deep,
The feeling hurt me but a gratitude
Rose up within me and a big upsweep
Of thoughts I can't describe but wish I could.
I felt fictitious, shoved into a realm
Outside quotidian experience
For grey-green light and mist to overwhelm
In a self-haunted, near-nocturnal rinse,

As of the end of something, or of me
And what I've done, and what I do, a stop.
Cool darkness shivered in that leafless tree.
A drip formed on a fern. I watched it drop.

A tiny noise. Water descending from
One leaf to another in the laddered air
And if you listen hard there is rhythm
To this belated rain on the green stair
Down to the damp ground, and it is as if
Water is careful, and leaves are careful too,
Helping each other on the leaf-cupped cliff
That is existence, down from the high blue
Through the green, and into the supporting earth.
To work this out would show me as a fraud –
All life's design as birth, and then rebirth.
It takes more than religion to make God.

Pushkin's Ring

He took with him a gold talisman-ring with a cabbalistic Hebrew
inscription, which Countess Verontsova had slipped onto his finger
one day after they had made love on a Black Sea beach. Pushkin
wore the ring for the rest of his life. It was removed by friends after
his death thirteen years later in a duel, and survived until 1917
when an unknown looter took it from the Pushkin Museum in
Moscow in the early months of the Revolution.

Neal Ascherson, *Black Sea*

Such is the history of gold, one ring
Appears a trifle in the greedy archive.
Imagine his friends' sorrowful smiles
When they tugged it over the knuckle
Or held it to a lamp or window, squinting

To read the lucky and protective marks
Which didn't save him from the pistol shot
Aimed by the foppish Baron. Lodged in
Pushkin's belly, the bullet left him time
To think and die, remembering Onegin
And Lensky in the snow, how poetry
Foretells and feeds on future sorrow.
But it's a splendid story, is it not? –
The real and the fictitious poet shot
By a literary, echoic bullet;
The glass-cased ring, which lovers, scholars,
Readers, peered at, curators' anecdotes;
A travelling poet staring hard at what
Commemorated Pushkin's seaside love
And lived against his skin like a woman.
Odd, then, that one loved by the people should
Find his ghost looted, but the desecration
Means little in eternity, although
I can't help thinking of its movement through
History, like those primary school essays –
'Adventures of a Penny', 'The Lost Thimble'.
In mine the penny went from purse to pocket,
Pocket to purse, from Duke to roadsweeper
And all round everywhere until it found
A beggar on Jamaica Bridge, whose life
It saved by buying him a piece of bread.
Pushkin's ring, too, could have been a godsend
To someone with a starving family
Or its theft commissioned by a connoisseur
Who craved to wear the ring the poet wore.
Pawned, hawked, or touted, it could have moved through
Revolutionary commerce, finding its home

On a tasteful Jewish man's finger, who liked
Its Hebrew inscription, perhaps, by now,
In Lodz, or Riga, or Kiev, removed
When lining up with others in a camp
Or at a ditch-side in a forest clearing,
Thieved, or threaded on a long string with others,
Smelted, made into bullion, gold death-bricks
Lodged in the secret vaults of Switzerland
Or transacted between God-knows-who
Among parked cars on a dark Alpine road,
A grimly European rendezvous
Where wicked history converts to cash.
There could be many other fantasies
Invented to describe what happened to
Pushkin's ring – for these things happen, not often,
As Gogol said, but it's a fact, they do.
From time to time, the answers are outrageous.
What you imagine could be true! Suppose
It found its way to Boris Pasternak,
Or Anna Ahkmatova, Marina Tsvetaeva,
Or Osip Mandel'shtam. Suppose it was
On Mandel'shtam's finger when *he* died,
And no one noticed, no one took it off.
Suppose it's somewhere near Vladivostok
In the ground, around a poet's bone digit.
Suppose Joseph Brodsky found it in New York.
Suppose *I* have it. Suppose I'm wearing it
Right now. For that would be appropriate,
Having lost another ring, having lost it
Because of poetry, being married to it.
Pushkin would understand. He was a good bloke.
He would have understood the pain, hunger,

Passion, cruelty, anguish, in all of it.
As long as he's remembered, he'd forgive
Posterity's Judas. He'd see the joke.

If Only

It was at a moment of Lambrettas
On Eastwoodmains Road, where I stood
Under a laburnum, waiting for her.

Rich kids revved on their machines
And I'd just finished work in the library.
It was 8 p.m. and the suburb glowed with prosperity.

I'd my raincoat over my arm and felt stupid
Not to be motorized or in tennis whites,
Earning £5 a week and working the late shift.

Dust on the pavement mixed with
Dropped petals and litter. A bee buzzed
In my ear, a yellow interlude.

It was a moment of swallows and evening sunlight
On the Tennis Club roof, a moment
Populated by sports cars and resentment.

My mind was far gone in lyrical grudges
Drowning in leaf-music and panic –
'What shall I do? What's my future?'

And she ran towards me, hot from tennis.
I couldn't believe it. I was so happy.
I'd expected to wait for ever

Or until a policeman ordered me away.
I think I'm still there, haunting a gutter.
If only I knew then what I still don't know.

You

You won't believe it. Perhaps you're too prosaic
    To fall for a poetic ache,
But your smile (when you smile), your eyes, your nose,
    Are far too beautiful for prose.

Don't credit this, my dear, if you don't want to.
    A poem, too, can be a pack of lies.
But if you don't, then I'll come back and haunt you.
    You'll find me hard to exorcise.

East Riding

'You wouldn't recognize the place. It's changed.'
For me, though, it can never cease to be
Outlandish shadows, all it was, distilled
Into five minutes' worth of memory,
A summary of years, unsought, unwilled,
Arising from unasked-for loping light
In which my mind is disarranged
And harks back to a non-specific night
Dated for 1969, and there –
A held hand, fragrance, leaves, a kiss, and air.

It's navigation by internal stars
On visits such as these into the past
Country, in whch the dead must reappear

Beside me, holding on, and holding fast,
Reluctant to be there, but ah! so dear.
The leaf-trapped stars are all in place before
Agog in-love astronomers
Who enter through a land's botanic door
Into themselves, with all of Holderness
Surrounding them, and part of their caress.

Some landscapes never change, because they stay
Unvisited as too significant
For a return, and must remain the same.
A stern but loved voice warns me off with 'Don't!'
And I obey it, drawing back from shame
To tell myself, 'No, don't ever go back.
Just let it always be the way
It was' – life-beaten, off the beaten track –
'The house in Ryehill that we almost bought,
And stars that in the starlit trees were caught.'

What happens happens as it has to do
And an intelligence can try, but can't
Succeed in finding out all reasons why
That, this, or that occurred. Recalcitrant,
All life can make is its domestic cry
Into eternal silence's untoward
Realm of the intimate and true,
The very meaningful and the absurd –
Patrington's pub player-piano, and tea
Taken in Hedon or in Withernsea.

Martagon Lilies

Here, then, is the painting, a sought-after
Botanical icon to commemorate her
Colourist philosophy. I'll weave around it
Invisible webs of pleasure, life and wit,
A vase, a table, a cool room in a *bastide*
South of somewhere Martagon lilies grow
In shade, a purple archipelago,
A wave of wonder in a world of weed.

Or white, as in *Lilium martagon album*,
Waxy and creamy, the least cumbersome
Plant in the world next to the Old Turk's Cap.
To chart its nature means scanning the map
Of Europe and Asia, from Portugal, east
Into Siberia and the Yenisei
Tracked down by an intrepid botanist
In sturdy boots, beneath a Turkish sky,

An eastern European sky, Mongolian sky,
Or in the Caucasus, sent out to ply
The tenderest trade, the study of the lily.
Only too willingly, too readily,
Would I give myself to that science of beauty.
I dream that one day I might come across
Martagons growing in a glade. Duty
Forbids such dreams, but I dream, and my loss

Becomes what Peter calls 'a piece of real'.
In my tweeded and booted dream, I feel
My way into a forest, and, in a clearing,
Discover martagons, my botaneering
Dream true in dream. Relative poverty

Prevents such wanted expeditions to
Far-off places. I keep my liberty
To dream myself into 'a piece of true'.

These are strange lilies. They survive for years
In wooded sunlessness, and then appear
When trees collapse, and light gets through to their
Bulb, rhizome or stolon foodstore, and air,
Sunlight, enough to stir them, makes them alive
Enough to thrust a spike of purple glory
Into oaked heat, shouting 'We can survive,
And darkness is only part of our story!'

Peploe knew flowers, and fruits. He knew them well.
Hats, drawing-rooms and ladies were Cadell,
Pure sailor-fixated, while Fergusson
Went in for the voluptuous, hard-on
After hard-on, full of the warm South
As only a north-man can be, café scenes,
Picnic scenes, curvaceous nudes, the wet mouth
Of his paint, and his erotic leans

Into a picture. And the best you bought
For the Ferens! Leslie Hunter's houseboat
And flowers fitted in nicely with your
Art-lover's precious optical amours.
You were so positive! I feel ashamed
Even after all those years of living with
Your taste in painting, and my own tastes maimed
By memory. Are you legend, are you myth

To me, that you should exert such a close
Posthumous hold over me? I suppose
It's all my fault. And Peploe's picture sheds
No light on darker truths. His lily-heads

Seem poised before abstraction. They'll fade soon –
The browning leaf, the blue, the white, the black,
Are all unplaceable. Is it afternoon
Indoors or out, or where? By what playback

Can I enter his eye? Is it a napkin,
Or folds of aesthetic white that draw me in?
What's that greeny black, that black, and pink,
That blue, that white? I look, and blink, and think
Beauty, not meaning, 's what I see, a pure
Picture of lilies in an anywhere.
I think, and think again, then I'm unsure
If what I breathe is art- or lily-air.

I browse the Caucasus. Oak-beech pastures
Of fern, in high country, yield my pleasures,
Discoveries of martagons. In chestnut forests,
I join the ranks of probing botanists.
The insufficiency of dreams leaves me
Fraudulent, a lily-lover but lily-fraud
In expertise, though growing them un-grieves me
With handfork-chink, weed pull, and hoe-prod.

Were I less literary, I might live
With form and colour, without narrative.
Instead, I argue. I can say a meadow,
Woodland, roses, and the colour of snow,
But not leave them alone. So, I adore
Peploe's de-vocalized melodiousness
And his infatuated eye, the *more, more,*
More of it, his vision's sheer harmlessness.

I've searched in it for meaning, but found none.
As for story, or moral – there isn't one.
I believe in the wild, and botany,

Forms, colours, scents, no whiff of irony
In perfect, perfumed woodland, in the leaf,
Flower, herb, meadow, and floral grasslands
Stretching towards infinity's *as if*,
In being kind, in the holding of hands.

Index of Titles